SE

The MULTIPLE STAFF in the LOCAL CHURCH

Books by

HERMAN J. SWEET

Published by The Westminster Press

The Multiple Staff in the Local Church®

Opening the Door for God

The MULTIPLE STAFF in the LOCAL CHURCH

by

HERMAN J. SWEET

PHILADELPHIA
The Westminster Press

Library of Congress Catalog Card No. 63-11562

PUBLISHED BY THE WESTMINSTER PRESS®
Philadelphia 7, Pennsylvania

PRINTED IN THE UNITED STATES OF AMERICA

To
Dorothy H. Arnim
and
Gordon A. MacInnes
for many years my associates
in a shared ministry

CONTENTS

I

INTRODUCTION

This book grows out of thirty-five years of experience as a member of multiple staffs and from many years of counseling in staff situations. Since 1946 it has been my privilege to serve the United Presbyterian Church in the area having the highest concentration of multiple staffs in local churches, and to be in a position to enter into a great many personnel negotiations and conferences on staff problems.

Nearly 50 percent of the 252 United Presbyterian churches in Southern California as of the fall of 1962 have multiple staffs, many with three or more ordained ministers and commissioned church workers. In the years of my service here, eighty-five of these churches have been organized, of which more than thirty now have multiple staffs. In the past ten years these United Presbyterian churches have called as assistant pastors 125 men directly from seminary and 120 assistants with previous experience. In the same period, incidentally, there have been more than 150 pastoral calls (calls for senior pastors). In other words, there have been an average of forty calls per year for pastors and assistant pastors. In addition, there are a considerable number of directors of Christian education, and ministers of retirement age who serve part time in various capacities.

To be in the midst of this volume of personnel movement, in a relationship to all the churches, is to have a significant vantage point for observation and study of staff problems.

I shall speak from the point of view of a Presbyterian having Presbyterian polity in mind. This seems to me to be preferable to trying to make the generalizations that attempt to fit all polities and therefore fit no one of them. If the reader knows that the point of view is that of Presbyterian polity and that which grows out of experience in the Presbyterian Church, he can make his own " translation." Having spent a number of years in interdenominational work on a council staff, I am not without knowledge of other polities. It is my observation that staff problems do not differ greatly regardless of polity, except perhaps that in the congregational type of government, staff assistants are less secure and breaks in staff relationships more difficult to handle.

It will be readily seen, as the reader progresses, that I have little confidence in the prospect of establishing fairness and justice, harmony and goodwill, unity with diversity, by any techniques, changes in constitutions, job descriptions, or other devices. We shall develop teamwork and some degree of parity through experience, through the growth of tradition, and through continued emphasis upon the nature of the ministry. We shall come to see the necessity of Christian men and women learning acceptance, understanding, and love in a framework of common commitments and common responsibilities as servants of Christ within his body, the church. The secular and institutional view of the church, which is an inevitable aspect of its existence in the world, and the human failings from which " calling " does not seem to provide an escape, demand love and forgiveness and dependence on the grace of God.

Already the image of the ministry and of the pastoral role is being changed by the presence of a large number of multiple staffs and by the increasing number of pastors who have had experience as assistants. Seminary preparation is being affected by the prospect that a large percentage of graduates will go first into multiple staff employment. Many of the larger presbyteries are no longer comfortable unions of senior pastors. A large and growing number of assistant ministers, sometimes aggressive and restless, and still, unfortunately, definitely " second-class citizens " so far as presbytery privileges and influence are concerned, are slowly affecting the nature of presbytery, especially in its committee performance. Though admittedly there are many problems involved, we need to hasten the day when there will be greater parity in the ministry. There is now a shameful jockeying for status, power, and privilege. We have a success image which is not worthy of the gospel which we preach.

The treatment may seem to some to be long on analysis of the problems and short on solutions. This reflects my experience that there are no easy solutions, but that guidance in evaluating a situation and suggestions for analysis are the prime requisites. I think that the careful reader will find many constructive suggestions in this book.

For the past several years I have had a brief paper on " Multiple Staff " of which hundreds of copies have been used by ministers and by laymen. That paper used essentially the same approach as here followed and it has proved to be effective. I know by long experience that what is set down in this book can bring readers new insight and understanding.

It is to be expected that what has been put down in this book will be interpreted by the reader in accordance with his experience and point of view. The senior pastor may feel that I have been too hard on him. The assistant may simply rejoice that so much is expected of the senior pastor and fail to see the beam in his own eye. I would remind the reader to keep in mind that I have dealt throughout the book with four main parties to the achievement of harmony and fruitfulness in staff relationships: the senior pastor; the assistant; the session and its committees; and the congregation, especially the teachers and the leaders of groups. Responsible attitudes and actions are required of all four parties.

But since there is a heavy stress on the more or less " natural " and perhaps inevitable liabilities of a multiple staff situation, and upon problems that the senior pastor must face as chief of staff, moderator of his session, and molder of congregational attitudes through preaching, it seems wise to make clear here certain points in my own thinking.

I have always had, and continue to have, a strong sympathy for senior pastors. In my counseling in staff situations I have come to bear down more heavily on the accountability of the assistant. In ordination the assistant has taken serious vows which demand of him responsible attitudes and actions in any kind of situation. If he desires the undoubted advantages generally afforded him in the larger, multiple staff church, he must set these over against the probable circumstances in a single pastor church of the size and type he could command; and he should not compare the multiple staff situation with some impossible ideal single pastorate. He may dream of what he would do if he were pastor in his " own church." I can assure him that many a former assistant who has become a pastor has learned the hard way, either that the role of single pastor has all the problems he had previously encountered plus some he had not dreamed of, or that being senior pastor in a multiple staff involves much added responsibility and many anxiety-producing tensions.

The assistant should accept the fact that his industry, his commitment, his attitudes, his relationships to persons, above all, his spirit of service and love, help day by day to create the conditions for his own ministry. Therefore, let no one read these pages simply to find out what circumstances excuse him for his own failures, or to find out how more expertly to blame someone else.

I have tried, as I have said, to raise the right questions. For most of these questions there are no easy answers. Upon all of us in the church lies the burden of finding the best possible solutions in order that the cause of Christ be not hindered by our pettiness or failure.

My correspondence and interviews with seminary students who are considering calls to assistantships indicate apprehensions concerning multiple staff relationships. They have heard too many tales of woe from disappointed friends. They may well discount these reactions of the men already in service; they are often the normal reactions of those who are having their dreams somewhat tarnished by the realities of life. Even though admittedly there are obstacles to be faced by any young minister in the best of multiple staff situations, these are certainly no more disturbing than the difficulties he will encounter in a pastorate. However, the bases of judgment are somewhat different. Fundamental defects in his character, personality, experience, or training will show up more sharply and be judged more harshly if he works as an assistant.

However, the man who has the qualities to succeed as a pastor should not fear the demands of an assistantship. Often the discipline needed for success as an assistant is just what is also needed for growth and maturity.

When one listens to experienced pastors, he hears much complaint about their difficulties with staff. It is not uncommon to hear a pastor say, " If what other pastors say is true, I dread the day when I must call an assistant." But we should learn to listen to these complaints with discernment. If a pastor says that in his staff there is " perfect harmony, no problems at all," look for superficiality and lack of awareness. I have known bitter strife to break out within months after being assured that all was well and then have discovered that the seeds of discord had long been present. Tensions are inevitable in any close working relationship that honestly faces the complex demands of ministry. Tension is not the regrettable fact. The thing to be regretted is the lack of Christian grace to deal constructively with tensions and to turn them into a witness to Christian love.

Or if a pastor is entirely negative about his experience with an assistant, he may reflect his unwillingness or his inability to face the challenge of growth and adjustment. The pastor whose church calls an assistant, especially a young assistant, has added a dimension to the demands of his ministry. If his ministry is now taking the measure of his assistant, the staff relationships are certainly laying a plumbline against the spiritual and the human stature of the pastor.

If we mean what we say about the nature of the church, about the nature of ministry, and about the witness of laity, then the achievement of multiple ministries which hold diversity in essential unity is today one of the great frontiers of the church. While we speak wistfully of the " house church " and other simplified structures for ministry and Christian fellowship, while we laud the individualistic and uniquely charismatic ministries, we nonetheless must continue for a long time to come to minister through large institutions which are never simple and never free from the limitations and failures that beset all human societies.

II

SEEKING TO UNDERSTAND THE ISSUES

Recent years have witnessed a growing concern with the problems and the possibilities of multiple staffs in churches. The rapid increase in the number of churches of sufficient size to employ additional staff is perhaps the chief cause of this concern. But the concern is accentuated also by a growing institutionalism, by a tremendous ferment in behalf of greater order in the church, by more integration and unity of purpose in programming, and by the rise of emphasis on lay activity and responsibility. Whereas in an earlier period the few large churches with multiple staffs were likely to be highly compartmentalized in program and activities, it is no longer satisfactory to divide functions into compartments and conduct them as loosely associated aspects of the total program. The emphasis upon the family as a unit, the emphasis upon Christian education as a function of the total church, that is, as induction into the life of the Christian community, and the accent on responsible adult participation, all tend to make of the life of the local church an organism that demands unity and coordination in staff services.

The pastoral ministry is judged against centuries of traditional practice. Whatever else he may do, the pastor is expected to preach, to give needed pastoral care, to call on the sick, and to have general oversight of his flock. Many aspects of administration are relatively new, and traditionally the pastor is not judged primarily by his skills in these matters. Although we may hear laymen complain about the lack of administrative ability on the part of the pastor, actually he is not finally judged by most of the congregation on his ability in administration. However, as we shall show later, his ability in administration is a crucial matter when it comes to working with multiple staff.

But if the pastor is judged by these more traditional standards, all other staff positions are judged by very diverse standards. These positions are not of long standing in the history of the church and have little tradition behind them. Ask persons who know anything about the church what the pastor does and you will get fairly uniform answers. Ask them about the director of Christian education and you will get vague answers, usually something about working with the children and the young people, or running the Sunday school. To most people the assistant pastor is someone who "helps the pastor" or works with "our young people." Most people have little clear idea as to what he is supposed to do. The pastor is not judged primarily for his administrative skills, but the assistant, especially the minister of Christian education or the director of Christian education, is quickly judged for ability in administration. The pastor may be judged by standards of more Biblical and theological import; the assistants are judged by more institutional and secular standards. The programming and multiple activities of the modern church demand structure and organization for which the assistant generally becomes more obviously responsible than the pastor has been while working alone.

It is interesting to observe that an assistant pastor will be criticized quickly for lack of ability to accomplish skillfully certain functions for which the pastor has never been held accountable. I have known instance after instance in which the assistant or the director was severely criticized for inability to recruit sufficient teachers and leaders for church school and youth work, often within a very few months of coming to the position, whereas the pastor had never assumed responsibility for this function even though he was well established and well acquainted with the congregation.

Two older pastors were discussing a young assistant. They praised him highly for his fine qualities. They spoke of the excellent response of their people to his ministry. But then one of them made the giveaway remark, "If he can learn to *promote* as well as he does everything else, he will be all right." I could understand the remark perfectly. The church has stretched its budget to call this young minister of Christian education. It is still paying for a new education building and it needs a new sanctuary. No matter what the depth and quality of this assistant's ministry, already abundantly evident, the criteria are still statistics. The assistant especially must show "results," and for most laymen this still means the tangible signs of growth: more members, more activity, higher attendance, better giving. If the pastor shares this basis of evaluation or if he is not willing to interpret firmly the assistant's ministry in larger terms, the "yes, but . . ." judgments will multiply. When evaluations that are primarily institutional prevail, an assistant who is sincerely and perhaps very ably attempting a ministry of depth and quality may become discouraged. At any rate he is not being helped to evaluate honestly what he is attempting to do, and he may so resent the pressures for mere activism that he will not do well even the necessary administration and supervision.

Some of the most unsatisfactory staff relations develop in churches with some of the best pastors, men fair and considerate, and very effective in their own work. This always seems to cause surprise. Why should there be difficulty where pastors are good all-around men, strong preachers, excellent in pastoral care, competent in administration, and known to be fair and considerate? Yet one finds situations in which there has been a succession of assistants under one pastor with each relationship ending in dissatisfaction on both sides. Incidentally, the disillusionment of young men who have come out of seminary to work with pastors of fine reputation, supposedly very successful as pastors, only to have a very disappointing experience, is one of the baffling aspects of this staff problem.

It is surprising, until one analyzes it carefully, to note that in some ways the better the pastor *as pastor*, the harder it is to develop a satisfactory staff situation. If the pastor makes a primarily "pastoral" approach to his ministry and tends to relate himself well to all his people, through preaching, pastoral care, good personal contacts with leaders, with boards, and with committees, it is more difficult to fit someone else into this total ministry. It is quite likely that the assistant will never be completely sure of his position and may come to feel that he is there not because there is a full ministry for him but simply because the pastor cannot get all the work accomplished. Members of the congregation, especially those who do the work, do not want in any way to be cut off from their minister. Our practice of seeming to allow the pastor to hand over to someone else any particular portion of the church's life and program creates tensions in the long run. It is doubly hazardous where personal ties are strong. It may mean that the pastor never really lets go of any responsibility or that the people never really allow him to. The members of the church may never really accept the ministry of other staff because the pastor cannot so work with his staff as to clearly establish status and responsibility. Neither sharing nor clear-cut delegation of responsibility is accomplished.

Furthermore, the constituency of a church cannot be divided into a number of constituencies. Especially invalid is our practice of implying that a director has a constituency of children and youth. There is no such constituency and should not be. All the people of whatever age belong to the whole church and deserve its full ministry. The director's failure or success depends, not on his ability to get along with children and youth or to work directly with them, but on his ability to work effectively with officers, teachers, and parents, the same persons with whom the pastor must have close contact if his ministry is to be extended into the life of the church. The pastor should never completely turn over pastoral care of any person or group to an assistant in such a way that it appears to be selective, and he must not assume that the administrative or counseling relationships of a director or an assistant pastor are a substitute for the relationship leaders desire to have with the pastor. The pastor's relationships are changed but not cut off. This fact makes it imperative to understand the differences between a shared ministry and competing ministries. Ministers in a multiple staff may actually be in competition for attention and loyalty of persons.

It should be possible to develop staff relationships that open the way for all members of the congregation to relate to the whole staff. The united ministry should be made manifest through each member of the staff. Members of the flock should find in each staff member a channel to any other staff member whose particular leadership or ministry meets their needs, and they should be able to sense that the care of souls, which they may have assumed to be the chief responsibility of the senior pastor, is in fact the central concern in the ministry of the whole staff. Thus, in a sense at least, pastoral care is extended and multiplied and comes to have many facets without being departmentalized. Nor is it divided into first-, second-, and third-class pastoral care, even though ministers may differ in experience and skill in meeting personal needs.

We must accept the fact that in the congregation, as in the family, relationships are dynamic. They are always changing. They are not the same this year as they were last year. Children and youth grow and change. Adults change. The power centers shift constantly in the church as new leadership comes to the fore, as new officers and leaders are appointed or elected. No organizational pattern stays fixed for any length of time, and it is fatal to the organic nature of the church to treat it as if it were a static social unit.

People will recognize and accept diversity of function, but they want to sense a wholeness and unity in the ministry, whether it is of two ministers or six ministers. They never want to feel that they are busy in a sideshow with an assistant while the ringmaster carries on in the main tent. Perhaps these are psychological factors, which are always somewhat in conflict with the necessity for the division of labor and organization, but they must be taken into account.

When the pastor " turns over " to an assistant any aspect of program, he may not be able to give the assistant status and authority commensurate with the demands of the responsibility that is assigned to him. Often an assistant is expected to carry heavy responsibility before he has had a chance to become acquainted and before he is accepted by the congregation.

Pastors may unconsciously treat assistants as if they were on trial. While not obviously rejecting an assistant, a pastor gives only tentative or qualified acceptance, waiting until the assistant has proved himself, whereas the assistant desperately needs assurance and support from the outset if he is to do his best work. If an assistant must prove himself before he can enter into the full support of a pastor and of those who follow the pastor's lead, he has a handicap that he may not be able to overcome. I think of two instances offhand in which young assistants are handicapped by great insecurity and a confessed fear of people. They find it difficult to meet strangers or to deal with persons who are critical or hostile. In each case the pastor has failed to discern this problem and has actually increased the problem by his criticism or his lack of sympathy.

A director of Christian education may be made responsible for a heavy program load without having an adequate status and the wide relationships that are necessary for enlisting volunteer workers. It is often noted that a woman director of Christian education may be brought into a church situation in which she is afforded very little more status than a church secretary. Whereas she is expected to be able to recruit the leaders for a church school and perhaps for a youth program, she may not have any standing with the adult groups from which these persons must be recruited. In fact, the activities of the groups are in direct competition with her for the time and energies of adult leaders. Often a young assistant pastor is given heavy responsibility with young people much as if he were a " baby sitter " hired by the family to relieve adults of their responsibility. If he is personable, skillful with youth, and willing to work night and day, he may have for a time what seems to be great success with the youth work of the congregation; but unless he is given the support of the entire congregation, he will fail in the long run.

On the other hand, the pastor's effort to be generous and supportive in every way may backfire seriously. Instead of really sharing the load in team fashion as the one who is head of the staff, chiefly responsible and in the prestige position, he may defer to his assistant in such a way that inadvertently he virtually withdraws support and undermines status. Said one assistant of a senior minister: " By repeatedly thanking me publicly for my help and commending me, he really reduces me to the position of chore boy. I am a minister, but he makes me feel like mother's little helper, all with the best of intentions." Said another: " By repeatedly disqualifying himself and deferring to me in matters for which I am supposed to be responsible, and by trying to build me up, he actually undermines the confidence people have in me and has the effect of giving me no real support at all." Said another: " He tells me I am responsible and must follow through with committees and groups, and he stays out of the discussion and planning process, but the leaders of the church always manage somehow to find out what he really wants or thinks, and that is what finally prevails."

The mind-set of the pastor with regard to assistant pastors is highly significant. Some senior pastors seem to cling to the idea, and foster it in their laymen, that men just out of seminary become assistants merely as apprentices, and that older men who choose to be assistants do not have what it takes to hold a "church of their own." We must establish the fact that in a shared ministry many may use their talents to better advantage as assistants and that many experienced men in search of some degree of specialization and a deeper, more satisfying service are now choosing to become assistants. Some recognize that they are more productive if someone else carries the chief administrative load. There is no doubt also that a place on a large church staff often affords more salary and more status and richer experience than a small pastorate.

A pastor complained that his young assistant did not get results and seemed to lack ambition. He maintained that he had gone out of his way to encourage this young man, to teach him, and to counsel him. He felt that it was his duty to afford discipline. The story sounded familiar. An objective look at the situation revealed that the assistant was expected to do two men's work. The church was certainly understaffed. The pastor himself was greatly overburdened. The young assistant was expected to give oversight to a large, three-session church school, to work with the young people, to do calling, and to develop a program of weekday activities. A long discussion with the assistant revealed not only that he was disturbed by the work load but that he was beginning to resent deeply and to resist the patronizing kindness of the senior pastor. He burst out angrily, "I am just as much a minister as he is and he treats me like a child." Obviously it was a matter of hurt pride. One must admit that this pastor had the best of intentions, but he had firmly fixed in his mind the idea that he had a mission to train these young men so that they would become successful pastors. This "one way street" approach simply does not work. There are increasing numbers of instances in which men who would be willing to continue their ministry as members of multiple staff in charge of education and allied activities become thoroughly disillusioned with their inability to establish a team relationship in which they will be able to have a full ministry while specializing in certain phases of the church's program. The matter of " second-class citizenship " for the assistant minister is still a critical issue in the church. It not only colors the relationship in the local church but carries over into the presbyteries and is a chief cause of unrest among assistant ministers.

This seeming severe criticism of senior pastors is not meant to be judgmental. As stated above, it is often some of the finest of men and the best pastors who have these difficulties. It probably ought to be suggested that some of our best pastors should accept the fact that their ministry is most effective in a one-man congregation. This is not because they are hard to work with or poor administrators or unjust or unfair. It is because their way of working with persons, their way of relating to persons, to boards, to groups, perhaps their too-ready acceptance of the traditional images of the pastoral office, bears greatest fruits when they work alone. Some are such strong " father figures " that those who are attached to them cannot accept another minister's leadership. In these cases the assistant may minister largely to the unattached or the disaffected in the congregation and eventually create a disturbing situation inadvertently. Some pastors will always be dissatisfied with the help they get and will always be disposed to listen to the minority in the congregation who complain against the assistant much as children in a family complain to their parents about each other. Their people will also be dissatisfied because they will feel that providing a place for the assistant seems to cut them off from the fatherly care and attention of the pastor. These pastors will find staff relationships a continual burden. The time and effort demanded for adequate communication and for the meeting of minds is a burden that they are not willing to accept.

Why will a pastor say, as I have often heard, " I never used to have these problems in my congregation until I had an assistant "? One answer is not hard to find. Often the unrest and dissatisfaction in the congregation had not been voiced before the assistant came. The pastor had not heard it because he was protected or because he did not choose to hear it. When an assistant comes, two things happen: the people voice their concerns to the assistant and they now express to the pastor these same concerns, except that now they have a scapegoat — they criticize the assistant. It is an unusual pastor indeed who can discern deeper causes and put blame where it belongs; he likes the scapegoat idea also. Especially troubled is the pastor who must have the show of peace and harmony at all costs. Though healthy tension is essential to growth and maturity in the church as in the family, he cannot allow such tensions. Now, with things being " stirred up " by more vigorous direction of activities, more demands on leaders, and more hope that something can really begin to happen in the church, new threats appear on every side. Some pastors cannot live with this tension. They are always seeking the assistants who can perform miracles painlessly and without disturbing the *status quo*.

The church is deeply conditioned by the volunteer nature of its leadership and its services. Most of the effort directed toward the upbuilding of the church itself, and channeled into whatever services it provides for its people, is effort given by volunteers out of the margin of their time and energies. Though other associations, movements, and organizations depend upon volunteer services, they are different in that the distinctly human motives of self-satisfaction, personal advantage, prestige, business, professional, and social success, do not need to be disguised. There is a false notion, which the church fosters, that pure altruism and "spiritual" incentives must be taken for granted in the church on the part of those who serve. They are expected to respond to pressures that seek to cover up the irrelevance or ill-defined purpose of the service requested. The constant shortage of leadership for the more essential services is a sign that something is wrong.

Now if the fundamental purpose of a full-time, trained staff is to create the responding, worshiping, nurturing, witnessing community and not to manage a successful institution, then their relationship to these volunteers is crucial. The staff's understanding of this relationship will constantly shape and temper its performance. And the relationship of staff to volunteers and of volunteers to one another is always affected, in many subtle and direct ways, by the relationships among the staff.

III

ADMINISTRATION AND STAFF FUNCTIONING

A certain kind of administrative ability is required in the head of the staff, and it differs somewhat from the administrative ability demanded when one is serving alone as a pastor. There are a number of reasons for this. One is that direct action and violations of the proper lines of communication and procedure, which are permissible or tolerated when the pastor works alone, simply will not do when there is a multiple staff relationship to be considered. The delegation of responsibility means first of all understanding what that responsibility is. It means being able to interpret purposes and goals, being willing to abide by the results, and being willing to follow through with the one to whom the responsibility has been given. This last is a significant point. Many pastors will not stand up and be responsible with their assistants for the results obtained when work has been assigned. Far too many readily blame their staff at any hint of criticism from the congregation or from the official boards, and are all too ready to side with members of the congregation against staff members without understanding the situation.

The kind of administrative skill that enables a man to

see the church whole, in all its complicated relationships, is significant. Perhaps the way to say this is that a man must have the ability to think of the church organically or as an organism, as composed of a highly dynamic set of relationships in which the health of any part is exceedingly significant for every other part. The chief administrator must be able to interpret overall purpose. He must know how to delegate responsibility without shirking his own continuing responsibility. He may delegate work, or allow the assistant to fulfill his function within a properly understood division of responsibility, but the chief administrator may not ever fully shirk his responsibility as head of the staff.

Perhaps one can highlight this problem by making the paradoxical statement that if a pastor cannot, while serving alone, direct successfully the work of the congregation through all the channels that are open to him, he cannot do it with a staff. A pastor's success is not generally enhanced by the addition of staff; instead, his weaknesses are often exposed. We shall return to this matter later, but let it be said here, for emphasis, that far too often the decision to add additional staff is based upon the mistaken notion that a pastor who is not adequate for his job can be "saved" by the addition of staff. This move almost never succeeds. It merely defers the final reckoning, often, however, at great cost in disillusioned assistants and recurring crises.

Administrative and supervisory effectiveness cannot be sustained without good communication. Good communication depends upon good personal relationships. Strained and inhibited relationships not only tend to cut off communication, they tend to falsify it. The "feed back" is warped or false. Neither side truly listens. Therefore, administrative decisions must seem to be increasingly arbitrary and often unfair.

This is the reason that the necessity for good relationships in a staff must be emphasized. It is not enough that persons " like " each other. It is not enough that they manage to be courteous and kind. It is certainly not good if they try to stay out of each other's way, avoid all tension, and merely safeguard each other's sphere of influence. Good relationships demand a meeting of minds, openness as to motives and intentions, mutual respect, and honesty. It is important to develop a high degree of predictability concerning each other. Staff members should seek to know each other so well that they make few mistakes in predicting how each may think, or feel, or act in a given situation.

This demands time, and a busy church staff is always short on time. Staff conferences tend to be crowded out. May we stress again that the usual staff meeting, while necessary, is often an utter failure for the ends we are discussing. Staff meetings may concern details of operation and become utterly superficial so far as any real dialogue is concerned. The time we are asking for is time for common study, for discussion, for sharing the deep concerns of life. It is time for understanding ruling attitudes and ruling " philosophies "; for understanding theological differences and the concepts of the church and of the ministry held by each staff member. It is time for coming to understand the family problems, financial worries, health difficulties, fears and anxieties, that color behavior. Within such a framework, trust and confidence develop, mutual support can grow, and the fullest possible depth of ministry be realized. Without it, the most important things that Christian leaders should demonstrate in the Christian community will be missing.

Let me repeat this for emphasis. Successful administration in a multiple staff cannot be indefinitely maintained without the good relationships upon which communication rests. " The spirit of relationships," said Reuel Howe, " determines the nature of communication."

In the matter of administration, it cannot be too strongly emphasized that a " mixed " doctrine of the church is the source of much difficulty. We have already indicated that a pastor is judged by more Biblical and theological standards while the assistants are judged by institutional and secular standards. These divergent philosophies are often in conflict in the management of the church. We talk as if the church were a family of God, a household of faith, an organism, but in administration and program we act as if it were primarily an institution whose mission could be fulfilled through the expert division of responsibilities, through executive efficiency, through correct organizational patterns and aggressive promotion. Sometimes the pastor will do his own work from one point of view and direct his staff primarily from another point of view. The pastor who talks most about spiritual values and who professes to have a troubled conscience because of the institutionalism of the church may be the most insistent demander of institutional results from his staff!

Corporate strength in the life of the congregation is even more important for a successful multiple staff operation than for a single pastor. This means that for church members, belonging to the whole has precedence over membership in and loyalty to various groups. If I were trying to evaluate a church before accepting a call as an assistant, I would want to try to sense this corporate strength. First would be the quality of response in the corporate worship of the church. Is corporate worship obviously a highlight in the life of the congregation? Is the preaching adequate? Are the officers and the leaders of the church regularly in the corporate worship? Does there seem to be a sense that this is really the pulse of the life of the church, indicative of its spiritual strength and of its intention and purpose? Do the teachers in the church school seem to feel related to the whole? Do they feel that they are supported by the session and the pastor, or that they are doing a difficult and thankless job without much encouragement? Is outreach a consistent stance of the whole church or is it the sporadic and unsustained thrust of uncoordinated groups and activities? Is " fellowship " a quality of the corporate life or a self-conscious effort of self-pepetuating groups?

If this corporate strength does not exist, one may be almost certain that there will be difficulties in maintaining effective staff relationships and the proper correlation of program. The congregation is not really united. It is too easy, therefore, for the assistant to develop a following of his own. Strains will develop and the staff situation will deteriorate. If we are to develop a group ministry in which, out of unity of spirit and of purpose, out of clearly defined policy, and out of commonly accepted goals and intelligently diversified assignments of responsibility, persons can function freely as a total staff according to ability and training, then we must start from this corporate base, this wholeness, which gives health and a dynamic quality to the witness of the church.

There are churches in which the present pastorate, and to a large extent the character of the church, is built on what may be called a " pastoral approach." In these situations, the offices of the church have been held in the right order, that is, attention first to corporate worship including strong preaching, then to teaching, to pastoral care, to outreach, and finally to administration. In these situations the pastors are administrators of a sort, but they are not *primarily* administrators. As least they are not "executives." They do not make an institutional approach to their ministry. The strength of their ministry depends upon their personal commitments, the quality of their life, their relationships to persons, their "care of souls." They may have all the "machinery" for the modern well-organized church and use it very ineptly. They are so strong in their pastoral qualities that the congregation will overlook lack of administrative ability. But these situations are fraught with danger for multiple staff. This is so, especially if the pastor will not recognize his lack of administrative ability, or if he has a guilt feeling about that lack. If he tries to direct his assistant to achieve an administrative efficiency that he has never in fact attained himself, he will keep affairs in turmoil. I worked for several years with a man who had become pastor of large churches mainly through outstanding power as a preacher. He had very little administrative ability but he could not admit that he was not an administrator. His high concept of the church, in fact, was very adequately communicated through his preaching and through his pastoral care. It would not have been difficult for a staff or for lay leaders to catch his high concept of the church. He could have motivated excellent order without the erratic and totally unpredictable meddling in administration that constantly marred his ministry. He continuously undercut his own high vision of the church by arbitrary and dictatorial excursions into administration, so that boards and lay leaders and staff assistants who caught his vision, and could have carried it into practice, were hurt and disillusioned.

A pastor who has the power of prompting through his preaching and general pastoral functions as shepherd of the flock his own clear vision of what the church should be, but who lacks the organizational sense to be an administrator, should recognize that he need not pretend to be an executive. Neither must he make the blunder of neglecting administration entirely. No dichotomy must be allowed to develop between the " spiritual " matters to which he gives attention, and by inference the less " spiritual " matters for which other staff and officers are responsible. He can make clear his concept of the church through his preaching and teaching and through his relationships, and he will find that there are lay and staff persons who can carry this concept into the life of the institution. He does not, therefore, neglect administration; he approaches it properly through his office as pastor. There certainly should be no conflict between the pastoral office and the high purposes that should actuate every administrative act in the life of the organized church.

A few years ago one heard much too often from laymen: " What we need is a good administrator." I think we hear it less often today, even though the church has grown as an institution. The increasing number of church administrators would indicate that this is still a concern of both pastors and laymen. The matter of the church administrator will be discussed in a later chapter. Suffice it to say here that it will be a sad day if and when our growing number of large churches, with their complex problems, cause us to exalt administration above the pastoral qualifications. The first call of a minister is to be a minister, and no amount of good and efficient administration can long cover up inadequate preaching and teaching and lack of pastoral care. Efficient administration may build great institutions, and has done so; it cannot build the church. This does not mean that a pastor need not understand order in the Biblical and theological sense. But he may serve the church well while lacking some of the skills necessary for managing the institution. We deal in paradox here, because the institution must serve the church. The institution is important. But there can be good order without institutionalism. Such good order grows out of the nature of the church, its mission, its discipline, its life as the people of God.

The pastor whose qualities and interests are primarily pastoral may be permissive and nondirective in administration. He relies on personal relationships with individuals to guide his ministry with his people. He guides his boards and committees indirectly. His status as pastor, the respect people have for him, his influence as preacher, counselor, and friend, are more the source of his leadership than his skills in management, in analysis, and in evaluation. He scarcely knows what an agenda looks like. He is reluctant to lead boards to decisions until there is an obvious meeting of minds. He is not very discerning about the intricate currents and crosscurrents of church life as long as things seem to keep going smoothly. When matters of policy have to be decided, he may seek counsel from a few trusted friends, and his boards and committees may come to recognize and accept quite readily his decisions that have been made through this procedure. It is not uncommon to find a church in which the pastor has long ruled by the advice and counsel of one or more strong and wise persons in the congregation, and in which the boards and committees, perhaps with some good-natured grumbling on the side, have come to accept this type of rule.

But woe be to the assistant who tries to discover how things operate in this type of situation! The pastor who uses this approach cannot sharply distinguish matters of policy from details within policy. In fact, there is no policy. Nor is he skilled in evaluating the effectiveness of leadership. His reactions often depend upon pressures. He is often unable or reluctant to direct a staff assistant. Now, just because some people in the congregation have been restive under this kind of administration, they are likely the more sharply to judge the assistant by his or her ability to organize and to administer the program and skillfully to guide activities toward fruitful results. The assistant has neither the status nor the power of the pastor, but he is expected to do what the pastor has not done and is not doing. This is not necessarily a bad situation, but it must be recognized for what it is. The director or assistant minister can never be as permissive or nondirective as the pastor can be, and get away with it, unless he is a master of subtle group processes and skillful at motivation.

The above circumstance may be more sharply highlighted when a director of Christian education in a highly permissive and nondirective administration seeks to establish the structure within which he or she can work purposefully. Then the pastor, who has always worked casually, informally, and in close personal harmony with his boards, but has never expected them to do much except to be a group of advisers, tries to deal with the demands of an active Christian education committee which is being stimulated by an administratively minded director. In such a situation it is not uncommon to see the floundering of the director and to hear him say: " I can't find out what he wants me to do "; or " I never know how far our committee can go "; or " He won't take a stand on anything."

On the other hand, there are churches in which the

administrative office has been exalted, rather than the pastoral office. The leadership has accented the administrative above the more charismatic aspects of ministry. These churches seem to be better organized and more efficiently run. They may only seem to be so. We can no more " organize " a church into being a redemptive fellowship than we can organize a man, a woman, and an assortment of children into a real family.

Under so-called good administration on the part of the pastor, the staff problems may be somewhat different from those under the predominantly " pastoral " rule, but they will be no less difficult. The so-called good administrator may be good at directing policy but very poor at delineating and interpreting it. Or he may make good decisions by intuition but not according to clearly defined policy. Or he may have a tight hold on things and give the other staff members no administrative pegs to hang on. He is sometimes epitomized by the despairing cry of an assistant: " When I ask the pastor, he says, ' What does your committee say? ' But when I ask the committee, the answer is, ' Whatever the pastor wants is all right with us.' " The assistant who, because he works with leaders and with groups, tries to follow democratic and educational processes in arriving at ways of action, generally with no clearly enunciated policy for guidance, may find the committee process short-circuited by fiat, or by decisions of a higher board that the pastor moderates and controls. Nothing is more fatal to the leadership status of the assistant or to the initiative and interest of lay workers. A highly directed, executive-run church tends to enlist in its lay leadership a disproportionate percentage of other-directed persons who like to be doing and deciding without having to think through why. They like the taste of power without the spiritual and moral discipline that comes from real sensitivity to the needs and feelings and responses of persons, and without having to think about purpose or about evaluation.

The strong administrator, no matter what his intentions, may find that members of his boards and committees are reluctant to follow an assistant to any final decisions, even about rather inconsequential matters. They always want to know what the pastor thinks. They want the word from the head of staff. I have known assistants, to whom responsibility for working with committees on certain matters has been assigned, to work for hours with those committees to determine policy and to outline plans, only to have policies and plans drastically changed, or dismissed with inadequate attention, under the moderatorship of the pastor.

Also, it is not uncommon to find the situation in which an assistant is supposed to guide a committee one of whose members has already conferred with the pastor, so that the pastor's influence cuts short the deliberative process. This is another illustration of the tendency to assign responsibility without making it possible for the staff assistant actually to fulfill the responsibility in proper fashion. One can see that this can happen either under the pastor who is not an administrator but who wields a strong personal influence, or under a strong administrator who cannot actually delegate.

We have already emphasized the need for strong corporate experience on the part of the congregation as a prerequisite to a most successful multiple staff ministry. One aspect of this is certainly strongly motivational preaching. The matter of preaching often becomes a critical question when a church has reached the size where it begins to consider a multiple staff. If the church has been growing rapidly and the pastor has been doing a solid job in all phases of his ministry, it is possible that he has neglected his preaching, or that his mediocrity in that respect has been compensated by his other performance. He may have been keenly aware that he has been neglecting his study and slighting his preparation for preaching, but the burden of administration and all the multiplicity of duties have been an excuse if not a good reason. While he has a close personal relationship to most of his people, they will more readily tolerate mediocre preaching. Since they know him well and accept him, they fill in the gap; they listen between the lines. They know how much he does and they make excuses. But as the congregation grows, two factors loom larger. The first is that an ever-increasing percentage of the congregation must judge the pastor by his preaching because they do not have intimate contact with him in groups and in their homes. The second and more important reason is that as the church grows larger and more complex, as it needs more leaders and more money and, consequently, deeper motivation, the motive power is not there. For in the last analysis, the one greatest source of motive power for the church is in effective preaching of the Word set in its proper setting of corporate worship. When the pastor obtains the assistance that he so desperately needs, he often finds it impossible to correct his habits and measurably improve his preaching. If he begins to take more time for study, some people wonder if he works as hard as he used to and some resent his "withdrawal." The teachers complain that the pastor does not come to their meetings anymore, and so do the women's association and couples clubs. He cannot disentangle himself from the "busyness" of the church and establish himself in the relationship that should truly characterize the head of staff. This situation is very difficult for the assistant, for it does not afford the right climate and the proper support for the responsibility the assistant undertakes.

Meanwhile dissatisfaction keeps growing. It is vague and unchanneled and does not center at first on the pastor, who is accepted and established. Instead, it is likely to center on the assistant. If he is a strong leader, he can hardly help overshadowing the pastor in many important points, which may cause difficulties, and if he is not a strong leader, he cannot establish circumstances in which it is possible for him to give proper guidance to the activities for which he is responsible. The situation is not uncommon in which a pastor who is not quite strong enough to lead a multiple staff, or to lead the congregation to the proper corporate strength for the effective ministry of a multiple staff, continues to serve a congregation that is vainly seeking to solve its problems in a succession of staff changes. Sometimes the vague unrest and dissatisfaction of a congregation will spend itself on one luckless assistant after another, or in switching from director of Christian education to assistant pastor, or vice versa, when the real issue is the inadequacy of the total ministry, as represented in the pastor and those who support him, and a consequent basic disorder in the life of the organism.

IV

APPROACHES TO BETTER STAFF RELATIONSHIPS

Various creative approaches to the solution of staff problems are suggested to those who have experience, merely through the process of analysis of the difficulties and by recognition of the high purposes that should prompt us in a search for greater values in multiple ministries. The frankness with which I try to state the problems and their causes as I have experienced them bears no note of cynicism. The outlook is indeed hopeful.

First, we must recognize that problems exist. We must see that these problems are not simply a matter of personality conflicts or of training, but are exceedingly complex. We must see the multiple staff as a relatively new concern in the life of the church, at least on the scale now facing us, and take comfort from the earnest efforts that are being made to find solutions for the problems it brings. Ministry in multiple staffs has only recently been intelligently faced in the seminaries. We must recognize also that problems of multiple staff involve laity and ministers and we must begin to help our congregations understand the basic issues in staff relations, colored as they are by popular images of the ministry and misunderstandings of the church.

Laymen who handle personnel problems in business and industry can readily understand some aspects of the problem of multiple staff when it is pointed out to them, but they must come to see that the standards of business cannot strictly be applied to the church. The volunteer nature of all the services of the church changes the situation in regard to the management of human relationships. However, there is the same need that obtains in any secular institution or business for clarity of policy and for the security arising out of understanding and complete sharing among all those who work together, both clergy and laity.

We must recognize that the ministry must be a whole ministry to a whole church and that all who minister, ordained or lay, employed or volunteer, are concerned with total program, if not in function, at least in understanding, in purpose, and in joint responsibility. It cannot be repeated too often to assistant pastors and directors of Christian education that if they are sincerely concerned about the parts of the church program for which they are primarily responsible, they must ultimately be concerned with corporate worship, with preaching, and with pastoral care, even though the pastor accepts primary responsibility for those things. If these elements of ministry are weak, Christian nurture is starved at the roots. If there are to be harmonious and satisfying staff relationships, each member of the staff must sincerely want for each other member the fullest possible success with his assignments. This begins with the sincere desire of the assistant pastor or the director of Christian education that the corporate worship of the church and the preaching will truly be the pulse of the church's life and the core of its experience. The assistant will truly desire that the chief support for his endeavor will come from those persons who are related to the church's corporate life in a meaningful way and not from the fringes of the congregation. Therefore, he will be concerned that leaders, teachers, and young people be in corporate worship, and he will be concerned that the pastor have every encouragement to conduct worship and prepare his sermons so that there will be motivational power for all that the church attempts.

In like manner, each member of the staff, no matter what his responsibilities, will be concerned about the effectiveness of calling and of counseling, indeed, of everything that has to do with the care of souls and a richer spiritual life for all individuals. There are basics in total ministry and mission that demand the primary interest and support of all staff members. There must not be pulling and hauling, competition and threat, as among rivals for power or status.

If the approach is to be that of dealing with an organism, the aim is that each part be healthy and that each part be regarded as essential. Persons may be involved in the church program in many different ways, but we still must deal with them as whole persons and not as segments of personalities. Each member is first of all a person with personal responsibilities in his family and in his vocation, as a citizen, as a neighbor, and as a friend. He has a right to be treated in the church family with due regard to his complex relationships in the world. Yet it is too often true under multiple staff that people are treated as if they were multiple personalities, one staff member dealing with them in one way, another in another, subjecting them to competing pressures which set up tensions and friction.

The attempt to build staff relationships on the basis of

an institutional balance of power, the deployment of skills, and diversity of function, without striving for unified ministry, invariably leads to trouble. So the first essential of good staff relations is not a proper set of job descriptions or a definite assignment of duties — which, after all, will not stay the same over months, let alone years — but is acceptance and understanding among the persons involved, and steadfast allegiance to a common overall purpose.

This achievement of a common ground for ministry is the point at which we are still reluctant to pay the price that is demanded. I have known men to spend hours together prior to assuming a staff relationship with the very good intention of understanding each other and establishing confidence and full acceptance, and then within a few months drift carelessly into a situation where each is going his own way, busy and preoccupied, with communication almost broken down. Time for cultivating good relationships has been crowded out of the schedule. Time for leisurely discussion and intimate sharing does not seem to be available.

Many staff meetings are almost totally ineffective in the matter of true communication. One young assistant said, concerning his relationship to an older pastor: " Oh, we meet and we decide upon schedule, and we laugh and joke and have a wonderful time, and we never get down to anything that is truly important."

In cases in which regular staff meetings are held, it is quite often true that there is no communication at any deep level. Following a sometimes perfunctory devotional period there are schedule clearances and discussion of the problems of operation and occasionally some attempt to come to a meeting of minds on matters of policy, but there is often very little that reveals attitudes, ways of thinking about situations, or insights as to more fruitful ways of working with persons. It would bring a new dimension to staff meetings if there were periods of good solid study and discussion, using Biblical, theological, and other disciplines. It would be valuable also to take some central issue in the life of the church and thoroughly explore it, together with its implications for every other phase of the church's program.

To focus attention on the " care of souls " it would be well on occasion for the staff to discuss some one family that is represented in several facets of church life. Sometimes a thorough study of an individual who is of particular concern to a member of the staff because of his particular need, or the role he plays, the power he wields, or the service he seeks to render, would reveal to the staff the superficial way in which they often deal with persons and the attitudes and feelings which each brings to his ministry.

I think of a minister out of seminary at least twenty years, a journeyman practitioner of his vocation, who in his busyness has allowed his intellectual fare to be largely printed sermons and magazine articles. He is a good pastor, a warm and sincere friend to his people, a responsible leader in the community, but his preaching brings the frequent complaint that it contains no depth in content and no challenge. Associated with him is a younger man, exceptionally well trained and with keen intellectual interest, who aspires to be an educator. It is not likely that the latter will come to do the preaching, but he certainly must have a concern that better preaching be done; stronger preaching is important to all that he will attempt in the other activities for which he is made responsible. Why should not this younger man be the stimulator and indeed the mentor of the preacher? Surely this kind of sharing is not beneath the dignity of either. After all, the older man has for twenty years or more given himself to arduous parish duties and community service and has a wealth of practical wisdom and experience from which the younger partner will profit. Nonetheless, there are certain limits already set upon the work that the assistant will be able to accomplish, unless something happens to the senior minister and to the whole congregation through a renewal of his ministry.

And certainly this will not be accomplished through the medium of ordinary staff meetings, the aim of which will largely be to bring the assistant into better conformity with patterns that have long been established.

True communication must be based upon something solid, which requires time and effort and persistence. The ministers must be satisfied that they understand each other even if they do not share exactly the same points of view. It is essential that they understand each other in important matters of theology, with regard to morals and ethics, and in attitudes toward persons. A minister who is judgmental and moralistic is often uncomfortably yoked with one who is willing to let love and forgiveness have their way, depending on the grace of God. It is important that those who work together in a staff have some common ground with regard to the ways of working with persons. If one is highly directive, and the other nondirective, they should at least understand the implications of these ways of working. Perhaps in no other vocation is one so likely to talk in high-sounding terms about democracy and to be so deficient in practicing it as in the ministry; and nowhere else is one likely to give more lip service to respect for personality while exploiting persons for reasons of self-satisfaction and success. Pastors are given deference and praise and power, and these do have a corrupting influence in human relationships.

It would certainly seem possible to develop a team or group ministry in which diversity of function is based upon solid foundations and mutually understood and accepted purposes, upon a well-defined doctrine of the church, and upon deeply Christian attitudes toward service and toward persons. Let me repeat, this teamwork will demand much more time spent in learning to know each other within staff. It means studying, planning, praying, playing, working together, sharing some tasks, alternating some tasks, creating a common mind and spirit, developing a high degree of predictability about each other. It is surprising how well some pastors and their assistants manage to conceal from each other their deeper motives and true feelings. They cannot face the hostilities that mar their relationships, because facing them would damage the image they have of themselves as true men of God. Much counseling in staff situations aims at interpreting staff members to each other. If each is basically insecure, ministers may work together as virtual strangers under the guise of friendly cooperation. Or they may be a constant threat to each other. It does not take much probing to uncover the hostilities. But the concealed hostilities, which cannot be faced, gradually undermine trust and fair judgment.

Dividing up the total job and staying out of each other's way, each listening to complaints about the other from members of the congregation, is no way to a shared ministry. When two or more men share the ministry of a church, each is certain to hear some complaints against the other. If their close teamwork and full support of each other are apparent to all who work with them, these complaints will be kept to a minimum. If good relationships are not apparent, these complaints will increase. If ill will, competition, envy, or conflicting purposes are evident, trouble brews quickly. There seems to be in every congregation a minority of people who delight in driving wedges between persons, and the members of a multiple staff are a fair target for these busybodies and gossips. If each staff member does not know the minds and the motives of the other staff sufficiently, he will compound the mischief by the way he listens to these complaints. Also, he will be open to many misapprehensions; he will tend to exaggerate stray remarks into a trend. Distrust destroys honest communication. A few malcontents who speak as often as they find a ready ear will speedily be exalted into a faction — that malicious " many persons think " which we substitute for accurate evaluation.

No one can be a true leader at any point where the responsibility is his if he must keep one eye over his shoulder to see whether his colleague is supporting him or is ready to pull the props out from under him. The basic insecurity that plagues pastor and assistant alike often lies in the lack of any common ground for trust and understanding. The terrific pressures and demands of the ministry breed insecurity even among strong men of faith.

One important thing to remember is that problems over details of execution would be minimized if we took time to establish and truly understand sound policy. When staff members are spending their efforts in trying to assign the details of program without definition of purpose and clear goals, confusion is certain to arise. Variety of method is creative only when common purpose is defined. The head of the staff has no business delegating work without attention to the policy which he understands and accepts, under which he expects an assistant to carry out assignments. Therefore, ministers on a multiple staff should continually renew their vision by study and discussion as to the nature and purpose of their ministry, and the nature and purpose of the church. In the complex organization and busyness of the modern church, it is easy to lose sight of purpose or even to pursue conflicting goals. Therefore, the church with multiple staff has especially to guard against becoming simply more institutionalized and more complex as to organization and activity, without a deepening of its sense of mission and without true growth on the part of its people. The more complex and varied the staff operation, the more clear and sound the basic premises must be.

Toward this end it is probably a mistake to continue, for any long period of time, a strict division of labor. At least there should be the corrective influence of shared projects and of alternating responsibilities. For instance, it would seem unwise for the minister of Christian education always to be the one to meet with the Christian education committee, thereby allowing the pastor to get completely out of firsthand relationship with this important committee and the work it represents. It would seem unwise for the various staff members always to call on certain categories of the congregation. In other words, to cast any one of the ministers in a certain permanent role may restrict his ministry, prevent the development of new skills, and be a disservice to the congregation. In one instance, the pastor of a large church and his minister of Christian education set aside the time for calling together in a sufficient number of homes to demonstrate to the congregation their common concern for Christian education and for the total life of the church. In another, the two ministers frequently realign their assignments. Another staff of three perform some duties as a team to keep fresh the experience of working together and to demonstrate unity. Actually, these shared experiences greatly strengthen their leadership.

Furthermore, a pastor's work load changes from time to time in response to the depth and quality of his ministry. If he is truly responding to a developing situation and a changing congregation, to the changing needs of his people and the stimulus of a shared ministry, his job description should be changing. And this is true of all members of the staff. It is true of long-established multiple staff situations that crystallization of the categories of work is a deterrent to creativity. If one staff position means always the same type of performance, there is not enough incentive for growth and developing skills.

The insight of the senior pastor is important at this point, for he will be called upon to interpret to the congregation total staff performance. Congregational attitudes are a condition of creative staff service. As an illustration, in one situation a young man was called to be minister to youth in a large suburban church in a favored community. He was called upon to deal with literally hundreds of young people and he proved particularly successful in guiding the senior high young people. Since he was never given sufficient lay assistance and since he was close to the young people, he soon had a tremendous counseling load, and since he was supposed to stay close to these young people and hold them in the church, he came to have responsibility for an increasing number of college-age young people. Yet in the face of these heavy demands, he came under severe criticism by members of the congregation because he was not able to pick up the same concentrated ministry to the oncoming youth in the congregation. The chief criticism stemmed from parents of junior high young people who felt he should be giving the same attention to their sons and daughters that he had originally given and was continuing to give to those who were now older. In this situation the job description implied by the broad term " minister of youth " actually was inadequate as circumstances changed. Reinterpretation of his role was needed.

There is a danger also that if the pastor in his administrative function is for too long a period divorced from the problems of creating and guiding program, he will become too " administrative-minded " to be sympathetic with the issues that other staff members face as they try to work democratically and creatively with the volunteer leaders in the congregation. He will forget what it means to enlist and guide volunteers. A pastor whose experience with groups in deliberation and planning comes to be restricted to the official boards may lose sympathy with the process necessary for proper guidance of many other groups in the church. In one large church the chief cause of tension within staff continues to be the Christian education program. The church calls competent and trained professional leadership for Christian education, but a strongly dominating pastor maintains the concepts of education he held twenty-five years ago in a small village church. And he is highly impatient with approaches necessary for guiding large numbers of teachers and other volunteer leaders in their service.

The problem of the relationship of staff assistants to the " power system " must often be candidly examined. It may happen that the official board members, who with the senior pastor evaluate an assistant's services and make decisions that affect him and his work, are those who have little firsthand contact with the assistant or with his work. They are in the position of relying almost entirely on the pastor's guidance or on secondhand data. Even for laymen who may feel personally that the pastor is arbitrary or "hard to work with," the fact that he is the "boss" is sufficient reason for supporting him against his staff, or for taking without question his evaluation of staff performance. And since in most situations the assistant is "hired help," judged by different criteria than the pastor, he has little recourse in case of disagreement.

There are other aspects to be considered. Does the assistant attend official board meetings? If so, does he have full privilege of discussion? Is he expected to express his convictions on policy? If the assistant works with certain committees of the official board, does his influence come directly to the board through these committees, or must he also clear everything with the pastor? Here, as noted elsewhere, much depends upon care in setting policy and in interpreting policy. Under clearly understood policy, individuals are free to differ in details; but when there is no set policy, or when policy is not clear, staff may not act freely without endless confusion and conflict. If policy is clearly understood by staff, then loyalty within accepted policy may be expected. Responsible committees and boards should be creatively involved in the making of policy that affects staff operations. Certainly staff members must not expect to debate their own differences on policy in committee or board meetings. But fundamental differences that cannot be reconciled between themselves should be frankly and honestly brought to a responsible board and not discussed carelessly with members of the congregation.

Situations arise in which it is evident that the assistant should leave. This need may stem from a variety of causes, from any one or a combination of causes. There may be growing incompatibility between the ministers, or the assistant may have proven inadequate for the task assigned to him, or he may be unsuited to the demands of the particular situation.

Whatever the cause, it should be obvious that lack of candor and openness is to be deplored. Yet often growing discontent is allowed to smolder, with both pastor and assistant pastor confiding in friends while allowing communication between them to deteriorate and to grow more restrained and embarrassed. One can only urge that they speak the truth in love, and prayerfully seek a working relationship as long as their association must endure, while at the same time earnestly seeking the way for a peaceful and mutually satisfactory parting. In far the larger proportion of cases when there is incompatibility, it is the assistant who should move, even though the weight of justice may be on his side. In contention with the pastor, the assistant pastor hurts the church, damages the ministry of both pastors, and jeopardizes his future. If by staying and "fighting it out," as some are tempted to do, he is able to win out over the senior pastor, still he has accomplished nothing constructive and he cannot remain in the situation anyway.

But when the assistant should move, the move should be allowed to take place decently and in order. Only in a small number of cases is precipitant haste necessary or is it in the best interest of the church. In most cases the church is more injured by action that seems to some to be unfair or unjust than by laboring for a time under the difficulties of an unfortunate staff relationship.

In one case in which the church officers were ready to follow the desire of the pastor for an immediate dismissal of the assistant, they were counseled to hold steady while the assistant was given reasonable time for a move, with the suggestion that precipitant action would cause much more trouble than the present irritations in staff relationships. It took six months for the assistant to receive a call, but the move was accomplished with no disruption and with no serious disturbance in the congregation. In not a few instances in which church boards have required resignations of assistants on short notice, satisfying their consciences with terminal pay to the assistants, the damage to the church and to the ministry of the senior pastor has been serious.

As I write this I know of three situations in which senior pastors have confided in others their strong desire that the assistant should move. In each case the reasons given seemed to be sufficient. A change would obviously be good for the pastor, the assistant pastor, and the congregation. But in each case the issues are not being faced openly and honestly, the reasons are not being objectively evaluated. When there is this sort of hidden and unconfessed tension, the lay people inevitably become party to the growing conflict without understanding it or without being challenged to give their intelligent support to a constructive solution of the problem. Often lay leaders cannot rightly evaluate a situation because they are given no help by the ministers who are supposed to guide and lead them. Ministers who find themselves in conflict within the church staff must talk openly and honestly with each other. If they cannot do so, they should enlist a third party. And unless they are utterly unable to rise above their own ambitions, hostilities, fears, and insecurities, they should be able to place first the welfare of the church.

V

CALLING ADDITIONAL STAFF

When the average urban church reaches a membership of from three hundred and fifty to four hundred the pastor is already overextended. There just are not enough hours in the day to accomplish all that he is expected to do. If he gives sufficient time to study and preparation for his leadership of corporate worship and his preaching, he will daily be compelled to make choices among a great variety of demands. He will neglect certain areas of the church work or certain possibilities for leadership and service, depending upon his skills and his interests.

In his book *The Ecology of Faith,* the Lyman Beecher lectures at Yale for 1959 (Muhlenberg Press, 1961), Joseph Sittler includes his somewhat bitter and somewhat out-of-context lecture, " The Maceration of the Minister," which drew much attention when it appeared in a popular magazine. To any harried minister who has not seen it, this lecture will be worth the price of the book as an outlet for his desperation. Careful reading of the rest of the book may help him see why he is macerated. But he cannot blame it all on present-day culture. Dr. Sittler's analysis of the predicament of countless ministers is painfully accurate. His despairing cry as a teacher that " what the schools elevate, the actual practice of the ministry flattens " is understandable. But that a trained ministry, especially in the Reformed tradition, armed with theological education and with the revolutionary power of the gospel, should so easily bow to these circumstances is not so readily understood. If, upon turning from Sittler's provocative analysis, the minister is not confirmed in self-pity; if he has a sneaking notion that somehow, somewhere, he surrendered too easily, let him read again and again the chapter " An Emerging New Conception of the Ministry," in H. Richard Niebuhr's little classic, *The Purpose of the Church and Its Ministry* (Harper & Brothers, 1956), and let him set out with all the faith and strength he has to reform his ministry.

It is indeed a painful thing to compare the high promise of the ordination service with the journeyman routine to which the minister is so often so quickly reduced, especially if he is an assistant minister. His " apprenticeship " is too often not in proclamation through the sharing of the disciplined life, study, prayer, and the care of souls; not in ministry of the Word in daily walk and conversation in the ordinary and necessary business of life; but in an endless round of necessary but incidental institutional routines, which are means little suited to the ends sought.

Nonetheless, the fact that he must try to minister to hundreds of persons of all ages and conditions in our highly complex culture makes those who understand sympathetic to his frustrations and occasional despair.

Of course, the three hundred and fifty to four hundred stated above is an arbitrary figure. I choose it as a result of long observation, without being able to substantiate it "scientifically." Granted that some pastors can minister to six hundred as effectively as others minister to two hundred, still, in observing pastors of many rapidly growing new churches, it seems to me that the severe tests of their ability to manage their own lives, to marshal properly their resources of skill, wisdom, and experience, and to work with and through others, become evident at the three hundred and fifty to four hundred mark.

If his preaching is relevant, the pastor's counseling load will be heavy. His calling will need to be restricted to calls that meet specific demands. He will have little time for general calling. This fact is in many instances a cause of criticism in the congregation. If he gives attention to teaching and devotes sufficient time to it, and especially if he is interested in leadership training and adult Christian education, he will have relatively little time for youth groups and for work with the church school. In fact, in a large number of instances he will already have a church school that meets in two or three sessions on Sunday morning at the same hours of his preaching services.

If he is interested in community affairs and does his share in the community, there will be many time-consuming demands made upon him by the community. His choices now as to the use of his time are crucial for his own professional growth and for the vitality and strength of his church. He is in great danger of falling into the habit of responding to the immediate pressures and actually leading a very disordered life in which much time is wasted in trivialities while more important things are pushed aside.

But, with the exception of rare instances, the church of three hundred and fifty is not yet financially able to secure any more than the help of a secretary, and from now on until the church reaches the size where multiple staff is essential or at least the point at which financial strength permits this "luxury," tensions will arise concerning the adequacy of the ministry.

In the single pastor church above four hundred members, the pastor's effectiveness depends not so much upon his capacity for work as upon his ability to marshal properly his own time and strength and to motivate and train lay workers. Except in favored situations, a church rarely is able to call a director of Christian education or an assistant pastor before its membership reaches from six hundred to seven hundred and fifty. Before this time, there may have been discussions at least among a few leaders and in official boards regarding additional staff, but rarely has there been the kind of study and evaluation and the kind of careful interpretation to the congregation that is demanded if the church is to make the right choice and be prepared for the rather drastic changes that will take place when a multiple staff is instituted. Still more rare is an open, objective, and informed evaluation of the aptitudes, skills, work habits, and attitudes of the pastor even though his ministry is the basis for staff operations.

Now is the time for the church to understand the motives that move them to call additional staff. The most important question to be kept in mind at all times is this: *Are we primarily interested in extending the institution, or are we truly interested in deepening the ministry of the church?* Actually, in most instances the institutional demands are the obvious and prevailing influences in calling additional staff. The points of view represented in the official boards and in the congregation are very diverse, but they are likely to be heavily "institutional" until much education has taken place. The temptation is to call additional staff and set them to work treating the symptoms of disorder in the church, rather than engaging this fresh enthusiasm, energy, and insight in basic reformation. An amazing amount of new staff energy is expended in making the *status quo* look more solid, and in increased effort directed to nonproductive pursuits.

There are some who simply make the broad generalization that "the pastor needs help." They never go much beyond thinking of the move to additional staff in terms of "help for the pastor." There are others who are greatly concerned about the parish calling. No matter what is said about this, no matter what lip service is given to evangelism, the real motive is generally getting more members; many persons are extremely concerned about the continual growth and the size and strength of their church without much understanding of what gives it spiritual power, and such growth seems to justify additional staff. There are some who are concerned about the preaching and feel that the pastor would have more time for study and could improve his preaching if he were relieved of many other responsibilities.

There are some who are deeply concerned about the youth work. They have seen their youth program go through up-and-down cycles incident to shifting lay leadership. Parents are concerned that their own young people seem to prefer the corner drugstore or Joe's place to the church, and they think the church ought to do something about keeping young people safe in a world of unwholesome influences.

There are many others who are distressed about the problems of the church school. Often the minister has had very little contact with the school and very little time to give to supervision, even if he is competent in this field.

The motive that needs the most searching analysis is the feeling on the part of church leaders who have been overworked and who have carried a large share of the church's leadership load that they are simply tired and need relief. Now that they can afford it, they honestly feel that they should hire someone to do part of the work. Unfortunately, it takes a good deal of education to bring them to the point where they realize that they should call additional staff, not to relieve them of work, but to help them to do more work with greater effect and satisfaction. Adding staff to do the work of the church so that lay persons can be relieved of the demands upon their time and energy is perhaps the poorest motive of all. We cannot hire enough staff to make a great church, and there are no doubt many instances in which the advent of multiple staff has increased the activity and organizational structure of the church without making any contribution to spiritual depth and to the growth of persons in ministry. Multiple staff has been a type of escape from the real issues of the priesthood of all believers and the growth of laity in service.

The pastor's motives in leading his church to call additional staff should be candidly examined. He should lead his people to consider critically the generalization that they are calling "help for the pastor."

Perhaps if he is a victim of fragmentation and misuse of his talents and his energy, "help" will be largely wasted doing more of the same. *The pastor will not be relieved.* Many a pastor with multiple staff longs for the good old days when he was "going it alone." Until he has had the experience, he simply has not dreamed of the complications that arise when he tries to adjust his own thinking and habits to multiple ministry and when he assumes the additional responsibility of supervising multiple staff. If he has not been self-disciplined enough to put first things first when he has been working alone, he will face all sorts of complications when he seeks to work with staff, and he will find that if his new staff help concentrates in certain particular areas, the work that remains for him is increased rather than lightened by the heightened expectation of the congregation and by the increased activities. But if he attempts to spread the "help" over the whole range of his responsibilities, he may find that there are more complications than advantages.

If he has taken the first course and confined the staff assistant to particular areas such as youth work and the church school, he will find that these areas are often ones in which he has been giving very little time and leadership anyway. Incidentally, therefore, these are areas in which he is least able to guide or supervise staff work and least able to evaluate fairly what is being accomplished. There are many instances where pastors have joined laymen in attributing failure to assistants in areas in which circumstances make "success" virtually impossible. Nevertheless, his people may feel that with the help he now has, the pastor should be doing a better job in preaching, in calling, in administration, and in leadership of adult groups. The advent of additional staff may simply expose the minister to more demands and more criticism of his shortcomings while giving him the additional time-consuming burdens of staff conferences and supervision.

There are two motives for calling additional staff that frequently operate and that inevitably lead to difficulties. The first arises where the pastor is somewhat inadequate and perhaps under criticism, but has enough support so that he is not likely to seek a change. Some of the leaders of the church may be motivated to seek additional staff with the idea of supplementing the pastor or compensating for his limitations. This is not a sufficient motive unless the reasons are frankly and critically examined. The leaders will usually find that the pastor's limitations are accentuated when he has to meet the demands of multiple staff. Often the aspects of ministry in which he is inadequate should not be met by other staff members. The hope that with additional time for study and less pressure of activities he will improve his preaching is often a vain hope. It is seldom that his administrative deficiencies can be compensated by additional staff; they are likely, rather, to be made more noticeable. There are situations where over a period of time there has been a succession of assistants in which one of the chief motives prompting the leading laymen in their search for additional staff is their desire to compensate for the limitations of the pastor. Although firmly entrenched, he may be simply inadequate for the size of the church he now has.

This latter fact is not always a reflection upon the personal qualities of the minister or his vocational choice, for in many instances in recent years pastors who have been adequate for churches of moderate size have found themselves serving churches that have grown to many hundreds of members. They simply are unable to rise to the growing demands of an expanding congregation.

Yet they may hold the love and respect of the congregation and may be able to ward off all attempts to get them to move, reluctant to give up the prestige and advantages of a larger congregation. Attempts of leading laymen to "shore up" these pastors by additional staff generally have not been too successful, and the frustrating experiences of staff assistants in these situations are serious.

A second insufficient motive is the desire of the pastor to gain additional staff as a mark of success and/or of prestige. There is little doubt that in some situations the chief motivation of the pastor to press for staff is that he feels that as a chief of staff he would gain status. He sees around him other pastors, with churches of similar size, who have assistants, and he feels that he ought to have one also. This motivation is a very poor foundation for proper staff relationships and teamwork.

It cannot be too emphatically stated that calling additional staff must take into account the whole range of the church's program and all aspects of its present ministry. As we have stated elsewhere, the role of an assistant may seem to be confined to certain duties in certain areas of activity and program, but he cannot deal creatively with any part without ultimate reference to the whole.

For instance, a pastor, because of overwork, lack of specific training, lack of interest, may have neglected his church school and youth work. But actually as pastor of the church he cannot have a full ministry without facing up to the realities of his responsibility growing out of the fact that he is the "key" educator. His preaching, his administration, his understanding and attitudes, so condition the situation in which an assistant works that the calling of an assistant for any particular function must also involve a redefinition and reappraisal of the pastor's role. If this is not done, either the success or the failure of the assistant in his assigned duties will ultimately produce more dissatisfaction in the congregation.

Thus the calling of an assistant does not solve the problem of the pastor's relationship to the whole church but simply makes it possible for a new approach to be made through a united ministry now enriched with additional skills, energy, time, insights, and training. The recognition of this fact is no deterrent to diversity of function but saves such diversity from the atomizing effects of institutional complexity and pressures.

It is not unusual for a church in a rapidly changing situation to maintain an outmoded image of itself and its mission and to continue to call staff who are expected to achieve goals and purposes that are no longer desirable or even possible. For example, a church in a changing community, worried about declining Sunday church school enrollment and youth groups, will continue to call assistant ministers or directors to serve primarily in these areas of declining response without a realistic adjustment of emphasis or of program. Identified in the minds of the congregation almost exclusively with church school and youth work, the assistant is marked for a degree of failure almost from the start. What is needed is a careful appraisal of the situation and of the program and the expansion of staff along lines that will meet new demands for ministry. A church that is suffering marked attrition from a rapidly changing neighborhood may redouble its efforts to do more of the same things that are already proving to be largely ineffective. It is obvious what this means for the assistant, especially if the senior pastor is a party to the illusion under which the church is laboring. In the case of a declining church school enrollment the statement may be made that " there are many unchurched children." Those same unchurched children would excite little concern if the proportion of children in the church constituency had been maintained. So also are there many unchurched adults whom the church is not reaching. In other words, to call staff to expand some facet of the church's activity without regard to the total situation is unrealistic. Any decline in any aspect not readily explained by a changing environment and a changing potential may be symptomatic of general ill health; there is little use in treating symptoms by redoubled effort.

VI

PREPARING THE CONGREGATION FOR MULTIPLE STAFF

When the church is preparing to call additional staff for the first time, it often makes the mistake of trying to satisfy all the demands of the congregation. In order to sell the need for additional staff and to justify the increased budget, the pastor and the leaders sell the congregation a bill of goods that cannot be delivered. In spite of the long history of unsatisfactory results with this approach, church leaders are still allowing their members to believe that when an assistant minister is called, all their demands will be met. So in spite of job descriptions and all private conversations to the contrary, when the assistant minister arrives — often a young man just out of seminary with little experience and maturity — he is expected to stretch himself effectively over a range of responsibility that has already proved too much for a mature, experienced pastor. He is expected to solve the recruiting problem in the first three months; he is expected to work with the church school, increasing its membership and attendance, improving parent cooperation; he is expected to become the adviser for the youth groups so that the tired lay advisers can have a rest; he is expected to help with the calling and other pastoral duties; he is expected to be on hand at the church day and night so that he can be reached at any time that anyone happens to want to call him or to see him. Since he is not preaching, it is taken for granted that he does not need any time for study, even though he is expected to be informed about resources of all kinds for the programs of the church. The sad thing about this situation in most instances is that the pastor is very ineffective in directing the time and energies of his new assistant and in interpreting to the congregation their teamwork in such a way that the congregation will come to understand and evaluate properly the services of the assistant.

From this analysis two suggestions immediately present themselves. The first is that any church ought to defer the calling of additional staff until careful study and interpretation has been made, and leaders ought to realize that continual interpretation is necessary because, in spite of everything, the congregation will fall back into its traditional habits of thinking. At least a year should be given to preparation before calling the first assistant. And the preparation should not be limited to consideration of the problem by a committee or by the official board. So far as possible the whole congregation should be brought into the study, especially church school leaders, youth leaders and young people, and leaders of various other groups. A small committee may come to a consensus, but if they have not interpreted well to the congregation, the weight of misinformation and misconception can finally breed great dissatisfaction.

After long and careful preparation, a church that had had a director of Christian education for many years called an assistant pastor. Through the leadership of the pastor and the session, it seemed to be thoroughly understood that the assistant would concentrate on adult education, the guidance of adult groups, calling and counseling; this understanding was in the face of the fact that there was considerable pressure for a minister to youth. It was the point of view of the pastor and the board that lay leadership should continue to direct the rather successful youth program. Nonetheless, within a year there began to be considerable criticism in the congregation because the assistant pastor was not working with the young people. Members of the congregation were saying: " We called this young minister to work with young people. Why doesn't he do it? " In other words, they had slipped back into their original thinking in spite of the interpretation that had been made. Continual interpretation to the congregation of multiple staff policies and problems is absolutely essential, and this implies that these policies have been carefully formulated in the first place, subject always to revision in the light of experience.

There is much to be said for the suggestion that a church defer calling an assistant until it can call two assistants, perhaps an assistant pastor and a director of Christian education. Enough has been said to indicate that there is a high probability that one assistant cannot meet satisfactorily all the expectations of the congregation, and it is especially true that an assistant minister responsible for Christian education, along with a wide range of ministerial duties, seldom gives sufficient attention to the church school. Therefore, any church calling an assistant pastor who is to have responsibility in Christian education should provide at least a full-time, competent secretary for him, or a paid lay assistant who will be virtually an " executive secretary " for the church school.

Corporate Worship Preaching	Pastoral Services	General Calling	Adminis-tration	Adult Groups	Youth	Church School
	Special calling Counsel-ing	On members On " prospects "	Boards Commit-tees Office manage-ment Etc.	Women Men Couples classes	Groups Choirs Counsel-ing Camp-ing	Parent partici-pation Recruit-ing & train-ing VCS

The above rather crude and inadequate diagram has been used to help lay leaders think through the problems of multiple staff. The main line represents the sweep of church activities, and the main categories of activity are indicated according to traditional organization. The divisions on the line represent in a broad sense the variety of demands to which staff must respond in the average church. There is, of course, no such neat division. There is much overlapping of purpose, of personnel, and of responsibility, and other things could be added.

It has been pointed out that crucial in the life of the church is its corporate worship and preaching. This is the first call upon the pastor. By and large, if he is ineffective in the leadership of corporate worship and in his preaching, the whole life of the church will suffer, and no amount of administrative skill or of fevered activity will finally compensate for the lack of motive power in worship and preaching. If the pastor is relevant in his preaching, he will in most present-day parishes find very demanding the counseling and calling load that grows directly out of this relevance. He will not be able to do general calling, which in many urban situations is exceedingly demanding in time and energy. Incidentally, there is no single point about which there is more persistent criticism of the pastor than his inability to do general calling, so firmly is it fixed in the minds of the people that this is a service which the congregation deserves. The notion prevails that, as the chief salesman, the pastor ought to be out selling the church, or that members have a right to expect this service or attention.

If the pastor is putting first things first according to his view of his responsibility, he will soon find that there are a great variety of " first things " represented in the points of view of his congregation. But as the church grows, he will simply not be able to give sufficient time to the church school, or to the youth work, or to the various group activities. He will not be able to be with the women in their association meetings or in their circles. It should be admitted that the average pastor should be much more adept at working with his leaders so that his influence and training extend to all phases of the program, but, nonetheless, he is simply not able to cover this broad range of activity in the average modern church.

As the church leaders look at the above diagram they become aware that help is needed in all areas, with the possible exception of the preaching, and that there is great difference among them as to where the main emphasis should be. Consensus will depend a bit upon the skills and interests of the pastor, but there will be represented in every lay group persons who feel that the greatest need is in administration, or in adult education, or in youth work, or in the church school. Each will tend to cling to the notion that when the church calls " help for the minister," it will be calling someone who will immediately take up the slack in the area of that person's particular interest and concern. If this point of view is not carefully considered and modified, the assistant minister will be under constant criticism almost from the day he arrives, for he is no more able to spread over this range of activity and responsibility than is the pastor, even though he does not have the responsibility for preaching.

The leaders of the church may decide that the most urgent need is in the realm of church school and youth work. If so, they are likely to think in terms of a minister or director of Christian education. Of course, factors in this decision are the wishes of the pastor, the budget, and the availability of candidates for the position. If the church decides to call a woman as director of Christian education and expects her to concentrate upon the church school and youth work, the church must face certain probable difficulties. One is that often when a church is large enough to call a director, the church school is already large and beset with problems of recruiting and training, parent cooperation, etc., so that a director, even one skilled and experienced, will simply not have the time to give the kind of direction demanded by the church school and its outside activities and also develop a youth program. Also there is the fact that not many directors are equally skilled in both areas.

But there is a further problem in that a director who is to recruit sufficient adult leadership for the education program and who is to be in proper relation to those leaders must have status and relationships in the total life of the church. Her relationship to the pastor, to the whole administrative set-up, and to the adult groups of the church will be crucial to her success in the church school and/or youth work. It will need to be thoroughly understood by the congregation that if the pastor sustains the proper supervisory relationship to the director, a considerable burden is added to his responsibilities, while he is not in any way helped with the work that has already overburdened him. In fact, as stated above, he may now find that the congregation expect a great deal more of him, since they have been so generous as to give him help.

So it is not uncommon to find a church disillusioned after a period with the director of Christian education and demanding that the director be asked to leave and an ordained minister called. Even though the pastor may suspect that this will not solve the problem, he acquiesces, with the hope that it will quiet the unrest and take the pressure off him.

So the church makes the change, often substituting for an experienced director an ordained minister just out of seminary who is now expected to accomplish all that the director has been doing plus meeting the demands of administration, service to adult groups, adult education, and probably youth work.

Just to state these facts is enough to make intelligent church people understand how faulty our thinking often is with regard to staffing a church. With the above diagram before them, it is possible to discuss the interrelationships in all phases of the program so that they are disabused of the notion that work and responsibility can be neatly assigned and a strict division of labor maintained. Experienced lay leaders, at least, can begin to see how complicated the problem is, and they can be led through this kind of discussion to understand what we mean by the unified, coordinated staff with diversity of function. They can begin to see what is demanded of the senior pastor in the multiple staff situation. They can be more intelligent in deciding what kind of capacities and skills they should look for in additional staff and what they may lead the congregation to expect.

When one watches some churches switch back and forth from director to assistant pastor without ever intelligently facing the issues that are involved, with the consequent unfairness to staff assistants and with growing pressures upon the senior pastor, one cannot help regretting that they are not making more intelligent approaches to the development of staff.

What about job descriptions? The weight of opinion seems to favor job descriptions. I have some strong reservations. I have read dozens of them, and most of them are so general that they are almost worthless. They often show very little thought or careful analysis. They are replete with such almost meaningless phrases as: " have complete charge of Christian education "; " assist with the calling "; " preach occasionally "; " supervise the youth work "; " recruit and train teachers."

Let us examine the last one as an example. In the first place, a new staff member is not in a position to do effective and wise recruiting for from six months to a year, except under the careful guidance of a committee and the pastor. He does not know the congregation; he does not have the necessary status. One new assistant soon had the church school stacked with leaders somewhat hostile to the pastor. Another recruited and brought into a strong position a " paranoid " who almost split the church and nearly unseated the pastor before he withdrew. Another with a penchant for sympathy for, and attention to, the lonely, the rejected, and the misfits, gradually had the program staffed with these good and most ineffective persons who did not represent a cross section of the congregation. That new staff assume recruiting responsibility is not only an unwise requirement, but a dangerous one.

So one might examine some of the other generalizations in similar fashion. For instance: "have charge of work with youth." To a minister of education this meant working with the adult advisers and youth officers. To the tired lay leaders this meant that he would be "adviser" to each of three youth groups, and all their problems would be solved.

Another general criticism of job descriptions is that they deal so exclusively in institutional and organizational terms; they do not define or describe "ministry." Perhaps this is impossible. But to allow any group working on job descriptions to remain at the superficial level of simply dividing up the total job without the further evaluation of all that is entailed in interrelationships, in staff aptitudes and training, in dealing with leaders whose needs, interests, and responsibilities cut across the whole life of the congregation, is to stop far short of creativity and fruitfulness.

To give some time and thought to a job description for only one member of a staff and not to look at the role of each member, or at the new dynamic relationship in service that will inevitably be created, is to be equally superficial. To write into the job description for an assistant all those things which the pastor does not like to do or does not do well is to dodge at the outset the meaning of a team ministry or a shared ministry.

I still do not go on record as opposed to job descriptions. In fact, they have been made a matter of policy by various agencies of the church. Therefore, what is to be said for them?

In the first place, they should be carefully worked out by a responsible group of persons in the official life of the church who have given a sufficient number of hours to study and discussion to understand what they mean by every statement. Either they should remain purposely very broad as only a general guide, or they should be carefully spelled out so that the ambiguities are eliminated as far as possible. Flexibility should be " built in."

The staff and the boards should understand that the job description is simply a " working paper," subject to constant study and revision. A church should never go out to find a man to fit a job description. Rather, it should try to find the best man possible and should be willing and ready to let him demonstrate how the description should be adapted. In practice, any creative staff should soon make all their job descriptions need updating.

Also, it would seem unwise, though it is so often the case, to work out a job description for only one job: the new job. If a church is calling an assistant for the first time, there should be by all means a job description for the pastor, and also for the secretary or secretaries whose functions will be greatly changed by the multiple staff situation. Introducing new staff without evaluating the secretarial situation has been a cause of much strain and much inefficiency. The coming of an assistant will increase telephone calls, mailings, office callers, and interruptions of work by leaders, young people, and the greater activity about the building. More about secretaries will be found in a later chapter.

Many pastors and most congregations have not given thought to how much the role of the pastor may be changed by the advent of additional staff. Six months with multiple staff will make a great difference in the role of the pastor, in the image his people have of him, in his self-image perhaps, and in his relationship with leaders, boards, and committees. A description of his present job and some thought as to what adjustment may take place would save much stress and help to create a readiness for a changing role.

A pastor who had had a long and rich ministry in one church had two or three less than satisfactory experiences with assistants. About to call another assistant and disturbed by the possibility of another unsatisfactory experience, he asked a friend, " What advice can you give me? " The reply was somewhat as follows: " You must look honestly at your own rich and broad ministry, your concept of your role as pastor, your ways of working, your relation to your people, and ask how and where another minister can fit into that picture. Surely asking him to find his own place in it, or simply to do what you no longer have the strength and energy to do, is not the way to a shared ministry. And your relationship to your people is such that you will not be able to divide the work organizationally; it will have to be a shared ministry across the board." After a long pastorate, especially, the senior pastor may be expecting his assistants to make all of the adjustments.

Too much multiple staff effort is directed toward strengthening or consolidating the *status quo,* and job descriptions may reflect this fact. Both pastor and church leaders emerge from the uncertainties of a period of rapid growth and inadequate staff with the feeling that with more staff, affairs can now be regularized or brought under control. Stability is preferred over creativity if the latter means more questions, more problems, more demands. The mood is not for experimentation and new ventures of faith — those ventures that may advance the Kingdom and unsettle the church.

If the concept of the church as an organism, best served

by a unified ministry, is valid, and if this concept can be understood and described so as to present a workable basis for forming a staff, then a desirable constellation may need to be studied from the standpoint of the complementary parts of a total ministry; in other words, the total ministry may be considered as a diversity of gifts with essential unity, rather than as meeting the demands of present institutional complexity.

For instance, in one situation in which the large congregation makes a multiple staff necessary, the personality of the much-beloved pastor and his way of working with and relating to his congregation have made it practically impossible for another minister to work with him satisfactorily. It has proved much more productive to complete the staff with lay persons who work with him harmoniously and with great admiration for his love and concern. To be sure, meeting the demands that fall upon him as the only ordained member of the staff subjects him to the strain of overwork. But the strain is no more severe than that of handling the tensions set up when he has tried to bring in another minister to share pastoral duties.

In another instance a successful pastor is highly directive in his administrative leadership of boards and committees. He sustains an affable and congenial personal relationship to all those who are related to him in the official business of the church. But as an administrator he is almost completely dominant. The obvious, the practical, and the institutionally correct solution to each problem is the rule, because he is a man of experience, good judgment, and great self-assurance. The " feeling " response of persons is seldom engaged and they are not led to think through to conclusions that they recognize as their own. Some more discerning laymen have been known to ask without rancor: " What is the point of going to meetings when the pastor's decisions, already made, always prevail? " These decisions, to be sure, have such a high degree of correctness that they are seldom questioned, but they are not mutual decisions. Whatever skills he has " in the care of souls," and they are considerable, are always secondary in his official administrative relationships. In these administrative relationships he more nearly resembles the popular business leader — the business leader to whose success his subordinates respond enthusiastically, albeit with some loss of a sense of worth and dignity.

This approach tends to gather into the church officialdom those who like institutional success. They develop a kind of pseudo churchmanship. They love to see the church grow in numbers. They rejoice in successful, well-attended activities. They like the balanced budget, with a non-too-severe scrutiny of the portion going to benevolences. They enjoy seeing the plant improved in appearance and in comfort. Whereas with this type of administration there is less continuity with the pastoral or charismatic role of the minister than we would like to see, yet there is much to be said for it. But the point to be observed here is that this pastor could be a better head of a staff if he could recognize the limitations that are present in his apparently successful administration and could see the need to complement himself by staff members who can work within the organizational pattern that he so ably provides, but who have much greater sensitivity to the way persons grow in decision-making and to the significance of participation in the activities of the institution as a way of discipleship and spiritual growth. He should desire to have staff assistants who sense the significance of group relationships and the kind of personal involvement that helps persons to deeper commitments and to responsible action.

The tragedy is that a pastor of this type may desire assistants who follow the same pattern and have the same success image that he has. This may be because he does not recognize his limitations, and because he cannot see that in his administration of the institution he actually uses people, rather than seeks to serve or to lead them. Or perhaps he cannot endure the warmer and more responsive type of relationship that such assistants may develop. If an assistant senses how persons grow in decision-making and seeks to develop group relationships that make for responsible participation, considerable difference in approach will have to be tolerated within the staff. The second approach differs in the time factor, and to some degree in the type of persons challenged and engaged. But too often the pastor sees this second type of approach as failing to get results, as too slow to arrive at decisions. " He doesn't get things done," is a frequent complaint. Especially will the " practical-minded " lay officers who respond to the first approach discourage the second approach unless led to see its value and to be more discerning in their evaluation.

These contrasting administrative approaches may well be reversed when the assistant is the one with the aggressive, directive leadership that is not in proper proportion with true pastoral concern. If these different approaches are understood and valued and made to complement each other, they may greatly enrich a united ministry. But if they persist side by side without recognition and honest evaluation, they almost inevitably lead to tensions, not only between staff members but in the congregation.

In another situation the senior pastor is an able and decisive administrator who could easily have been a leader in any profession. As the head of a large staff he leaves no doubt as to his role as chief administrator, but at the same time he is never bogged down with details. He can delineate and clarify policy with boards and committees and interpret policy to the staff so that they may act responsibly with a minimum of supervision, but with no sense of being isolated. He gives time to study and to his preaching, in which he excels. He is a community leader without being subservient to trivial demands. Whereas his door is never closed to those who need his counsel, he obviously has very limited time and energy for routine pastoral duties. It is fortunate, therefore, that he sees the importance of having on his staff an assistant pastor of great charismatic gifts: a man with great sensitivity to persons, a man who radiates love and gentleness, a man mature and secure so that he does not need to cultivate status or honor for himself. And it is a joy to see how each of these men loves and respects and trusts the other so as actually to complement each other without a hint of jealousy or rivalry. In responding to one man, no parishioner would ever be likely to feel disloyal to the other or feel any conflict of loyalties. This is as it should be, but it must be admitted that it takes men of stature to achieve this kind of harmony in ministry.

These latter cases are but a few of the examples that might be outlined to indicate the kind of analysis that pastors should make, and that they may well guide their boards and committees to make, as they face the process of forming a church staff.

VII

DISTAFF

This chapter will be devoted to the women: wives, secretaries, and directors of Christian education. No consideration of staff problems would be complete without a look at the place of these highly important persons in the pastor's life and work.

I shall use some well-disguised illustrations; that is, these shoes would fit so many persons it is of little use to try them on for size.

The role of the *minister's wife* is a difficult role to play. She lives in a glass house. Her attitudes, her appearance, her management of her family, her social contacts, are all subject to severe scrutiny. And when it comes to participation in the life of the congregation, she is damned if she does and damned if she does not. It is little wonder so many ministers' wives are under psychiatric care.

In an evaluation of staff relationships, the attitudes and the influence of wives is often the most important " hidden " factor. In one large church with three assistant ministers, the pastor's wife never assumed any leadership of any kind in church activities, except, of course, to be faithful in attendance. Therefore, it was a rule that no assistant's wife would accept any leadership responsibility. In more than twenty years, and through a long succession of assistants, the name of an assistant's wife never appeared in any church publication. No matter how able, no one of them ever taught, led a devotional for the women, or served in any way. This is one way to meet the question of the participation of pastors' wives.

Contrast with this the situations where the pastor's wife is a dominant factor in the life of the church. One pastor had a succession of assistants. Each one left highly dissatisfied. In each case the most pointed reason was never openly discussed. The pastor's wife had a strong image of herself as the ideal pastor's wife. For good or bad her husband shared this opinion. In each case she set out to direct the assistant's wife: her activity in the church, her care of her children and of her home, her dress, and her general behavior. Result: resentment and finally revolt. Around this " hidden " agenda gathered other conflicts that otherwise could have been resolved.

In another long pastorate with a record of disturbed staff relationships, the pastor's wife was an exceedingly able, though rigid and inflexible, leader. She was firmly entrenched in the church school as head of " Mrs. ———'s Department." She enlisted her own " helpers." Her department never changed, and was the church school norm for the congregation. Directors or ministers of Christian education worked around it as best they could. The one D.C.E. who called for a showdown as to whether she or the pastor's wife was director had a very short tenure! Active in all phases of the church life and dominant in her influence over her husband, this strong and able woman was in a well-mannered contest with every assistant, and she always won. The complaints of the troublemakers and the dissatisfied came to her. She kept her faithful husband running about trying to put out these little fires. By the time he had done so, no assistant or director had any status or influence left. And this fine man, who wanted nothing so much as successful staff relationships, could never quite understand why he failed.

And so we have the nonparticipating wife and the deeply involved wife. There is also the protective wife, self-appointed guardian of her husband's status, health, and supposed prerogatives as the pastor. She is immediately on guard if the problems of staff add to her husband's anxieties, as they often do. She is especially sensitive if the assistant seems to be winning a place for himself or is given any praise. She sees in the assistant a rival and she will find ways to undermine him. I have heard more than one wife say with some bitterness: "This extra staff was supposed to help my husband, but he has more worry and work than ever before."

Or the protective wife may be the assistant's wife. Not having satisfactory status in the church, she may be overly solicitous for her husband, or exceedingly jealous of his time. One assistant's wife insisted that he have an after-lunch nap, especially on days when he had evening meetings. When parishioners would call the church, a not-too-friendly secretary would suggest that they call him at home. His wife would reply that he was resting and could not be disturbed. But why go on? He did not last out the year! Fortunately, a counselor was able to help him to see that this pattern must be changed. An overly protective wife, always talking about how her husband is overworked or how tired he is, or how no one appreciates how hard he works, can alienate much goodwill.

There is another type of pastor's wife who is a great trial to assistants. It is the wife who is very able as a leader but is a star performer. Often she will plunge in until she is over her head and then withdraw, sometimes on "doctor's orders," leaving some phase of the program a shambles. The assistant is the one to pick up the pieces, and he often inherits the blame since her position protects her. While she is getting sympathy for "nervous exhaustion," the assistant takes the blame for failure of the activity or group that was built around her.

In one situation the pastor's wife was especially adept at building up an adult class in the church school. Among its members were those who should have been teaching children and youth. During her husband's pastorate in one church, ministers of Christian education came and went. One of the chief difficulties in each case was inability to enlist leadership. The pastor's wife was the chief competitor! No one dared challenge her drive for a large adult class.

Sometimes in what appears to be a beautifully shared life, the pastor's wife is a strong or dominant influence in all of his judgments and decisions. Boards and committees come to understand that any agreement may be reinterpreted after the pastor has conferred with his wife. Said an assistant: "I have learned never to count anything settled until she has passed judgment on it." In more than one case, the director or an assistant has had to reckon with the fact that the pastor's wife maintained relationships with key leaders and always outranked him in influence.

Enough has been said to alert pastors, or those about to become assistants, or personnel committees, to the reality of this phase of staff relationships. Senior pastors need to be a great deal more honest in recognizing the role of their wives and perhaps a great deal more discerning in sizing up the wife of a prospective assistant. The oft-repeated statement, " After all, we are not hiring the wife," settles just exactly nothing at all.

The fact that many assistants are married during their seminary years, and often even in college, adds to the problem. Many wives have taken some seminary training or have worked along with their husbands on student jobs. They have not counted on having to take second place or having to feel their way in competition with a pastor's wife who is already firmly established. Many also have held responsible positions. They have been the chief breadwinners, often virtually the heads of families, while the husbands have been students. Because of training and experience, they have skills that the pastor's wife may not have. But they had better be tactful about using these skills, at least until they are aware of the implications.

All committees should interview wives as well as candidates. It is not enough, generally, for the ministers to confer; the families should meet also before a call is issued. A minister being considered for a call as assistant should be alert for certain signs. One sign is the frequency with which a pastor may quote his wife or refer to her opinion. Another is her tendency when they are together to " explain " her husband or to interpret what he is saying. Another is any evidence that she considers herself an expert in any one phase of program, such as teaching, or youth work, or music. Given any of these signs, I would want the more carefully to evaluate the situation.

The increasing number of cases in which a minister leaves a pastorate to become an associate or an assistant calls for the warning that this is often a severe test for wife and family. From leading role to second place may be a difficult transition. The radically changed position of the minister himself affects family life drastically. He is no longer as free, and his status is not the same. His family shares this changed status, and it often gives rise to tensions.

Do not be misled. I have a high regard for ministers' wives. After all, I have been married to one for over forty years!

The *church secretary,* and particularly the pastor's secretary if there is a multiple office force, is a key person in staff relations.

In some situations the secretary wields great power and influence. She may be widely acquainted in the congregation. She commands that powerful instrument, the telephone. She meets and talks with those who come to the church office. She is often the leading public relations personage on the staff.

Sometimes she is fiercely loyal to the pastor and resents the intrusion of another staff member. She also resents the extra work that may be entailed. The secretary handles many communications between staff members. She may slant them both ways. A *suggestion* by the pastor may become an *order* that she delivers. A chance remark of an assistant becomes a mark of disloyalty or disrespect. Telephone messages are slightly garbled when relayed, or else are forgotten.

In cases where the assistant has his own secretary, relationship between secretaries is highly important. Their rivalry, jealousy, or intrigue can be subtly reflected in staff relationships, and only frank and open facing of the problems will prevent trouble. The fact that some pastors come to accept with little question the judgments and the evaluations of their secretaries in all matters, even where they have no competency, is amazing, to say the least. In cases where a pastor's secretary makes of him a little tin god, protects him, flatters him, and controls his appointments and commitments, assistants should beware. When misunderstandings arise and the relationship goes sour, the real reason will seldom be mentioned. The secretary is indispensable and invulnerable! Her next victim will be along soon.

A good secretary is almost a necessity for the pastor, especially in a church large enough to have multiple staff. A strong secretary becomes virtually an assistant, a " right-hand man." Even if the pastor comes to recognize or admit that she practically " runs the church " in those numerous instances where this happens, he is already so dependent on her help, her judgment, her protection, and her loyalty and devotion that he will usually defend her against other staff. Many an assistant or director has suffered the handicap of having his performance interpreted and evaluated for the pastor largely through the subtle influences of a secretary.

Any committee or board representing a congregation in calling an assistant pastor or a director of Christian education should carefully evaluate the secretarial services available. If there is not sufficient secretarial service, either the assistant will be spending time doing his own secretarial work when he should be doing other things, or he will be competing for services from a secretary who probably is already overburdened or considers herself to be. Since the established work load has first call, he is at a great disadvantage, and a cause for friction has been introduced. Adjustments in secretarial services must be considered in any staff expansion at the outset.

As I write this, I am aware that three *directors of Christian education* have been asked to resign within the past month in one presbytery. The reasons differ. But the fact of job insecurity is shockingly pointed up, for in not one of these three cases would an objective evaluation justify the action.

In one case it is the familiar pattern: a good director who admittedly has done an excellent job with church school and youth is being sacrificed because some church officers want an ordained man. So they will exchange an experienced director for a man just out of seminary who will be expected to do all that she is doing plus "helping the pastor," whatever that means. He will fail in large measure. Unless he is exceptional, he will be happy to leave within two years.

In a second instance, the pastor is involved in discord in the church so that he is forced to leave. The director is caught in the turmoil, the victim of much misdirected criticism and aimless frustration. In a third instance, the persistent, and largely unjustified, opposition of a few lay leaders causes the harassed and annoyed pastor to settle the argument by removing the "cause." The trouble is that nothing is really settled, the real issues are not met.

Thirty years of counseling with directors leaves me perplexed about the role of the woman director. The demand seems to exceed the supply, but it is a hazardous profession, to say the least, and after all the attempts at job descriptions and countless attempts to define the role of a D.C.E., the picture is clouded, indeed.

Perhaps it will be profitable to suggest a few problem areas.

In the first place, most women directors have a primary responsibility in the church school. The pastor and the official boards seldom understand what is involved in properly directing a modern church school, especially in a multiple staff church, which may have a large school, meeting in two or three sections. If the director fulfills the expectations of teachers and parents and if she gives educational guidance and not merely the complicated administrative oversight that is demanded, she has an exacting and time-consuming job. The time demand alone is often greatly underestimated.

If then she must fight for the support of the entire church, which is so necessary to a successful educational program, and if she must win for herself the status and " authority " commensurate with her responsibilities, she is in an uphill pull.

Only a few directors are equally effective in youth work and in the church school and its related activities. And those who can do both have not the time and energy to do both, except in cases of exceptional support from the pastor and the lay leadership of the church. More often than not, lack of success with youth is one of the chief complaints against the director.

Recently a director considering a new position was told that her work would be strictly " children's work "; there will be a " minister to youth " on the staff. Of course, it is not " children's work." It is work with a large number of adults who work with children in a very large church school. The kind of thinking that allows pastor and committee to refer to this as " children's work " and to consider the D.C.E. as a " children's worker " probably implies an inadequate concept of the place a director must have in the total church in order to sustain the responsibility for recruiting and training that will be hers. If there is not good staff and total program integration, any apparent ultimate success will be at the cost of compartmentalization and of recruiting from the fringes of the congregation. That is why so often in the past an excellent church school turned out to be not a school of the church but a semi-independent organization.

The seminaries have come to expect a good percentage of women students to marry ministerial students. For those who do not, some question is raised at once concerning emotional maturity, social adjustment, and personality. The single woman may come out of seminary with some deep misgivings about herself. When she gets to her first position, still young and relatively inexperienced, so much is expected of her all at once that her self-confidence is severely tested. No matter how able she is, she simply cannot meet the demands made upon her by a congregation having a complex and clouded picture of what her functions are. Her success will depend very largely on the wisdom and patience of the pastor. This relationship of pastor and D.C.E. is difficult to discuss. She may have been advised to work closely with the pastor, and he may for a time accept this responsibility, but she may lean too heavily, and expect so much support that he begins to withdraw. This " rejection " may be very disturbing. Many a pastor has grown tired or wary of being the " security figure " for a lonely single woman and has been happy to have her move on. She will report in some bewilderment that he was at first very helpful and friendly but withdrew his support.

A pastor is ill-advised who turns Christian education over to a director. If he is able to supervise the educational activities as a part of his total ministry, a director working with him can be effective. This support of pastor and of the boards that he guides can make for integrated or correlated program, and make it possible for the director to succeed. But a director expected to make it on her own in a compartmentalized program usually ultimately will fail. She does not have the contacts and status to sustain her heavy responsibilities. She may be so cut off from the " power structure " that support is lacking. Also, the means of proper evaluation and of interpretation to the congregation is lacking.

The satisfactory service of lay women as assistants to the ministers with major responsibility for the direction of the church school is worth examining. These persons often have had some public-school training and experience. They may have raised a family. They may have been successful homemakers, but now find the time to develop a career, at least part time. Or they may be widows and in some cases women whose marriage has failed. They generally have a lifelong experience in the church and have availed themselves of more or less informal training. They are likely to be emotionally mature, socially secure, with many practical skills developed over the years. They have had enough worldly experience to pretty accurately size up a minister and to adjust their relationships so as not to threaten him or to try his patience.

No amount of academic preparation can compensate for lack of these qualities. Given these qualities and a capacity for growth, these women learn rapidly on the job and from those opportunities for informal training that are now afforded in the church and in the community. Experience with these lay leaders indicates that we should look again at the possibility of recruiting these persons in greater numbers and providing for them not only short courses in college and seminary, perhaps with liberal scholarship aid, but increasing opportunities for training on the job and in short-term schools and institutes.

With regard to young women who wish to train for careers in the local church, one thing to be said is that those charged with the guidance and supervision of church vocation candidates, and admission officers of seminaries, should improve their screening so that women who are unsuited for this difficult profession because of emotional instability or personality problems will be guided into other vocations. Certainly a number of young women are graduated each year who are years away in maturity and experience from being competent to face the exacting demands made upon educators in the church. This may mean that young women who have a sense of being called to a career in the church as educators should be encouraged to get some years of practical experience in business or in public education, preferably before they go to seminary. With our present system of selection and training there are far too many disappointments. I am skirting the question of ordination for women because I feel that I have no settled convictions in the matter, but at present I cannot see that ordination, except in the case of a few women who may become pastors, will settle any of the problems that we now face in staff relationships.

If I were a pastor of a church calling a young woman with seminary training in Christian education, I would rather that she would be called as assistant to the minister. This would imply that the pastor is " director " of the total program and remains so. The title " Director of Christian Education " implies a proficiency and a responsibility that is generally beyond her until she has had years of maturing experience. Unless the young director is exceptional in her ability to work with adults, exceptional in administrative and supervisory ability and as a teacher, she will need to serve within a framework of administrative oversight and supportive direction provided by the minister and the boards and committees whose interest and active engagement he only is in a position to enlist. Of the women directors whom I have known who have left the profession, there are some who could have become very effective if a different set of demands had been placed upon them. For example, one director was frequently praised by the pastor for her teaching and counseling skills. But she was an utter failure as an administrator. If the pastor, the director, and the congregation had not had so fixed an image of her as administrator of the church school and youth program, she could have continued to make a rich contribution to the total work of the parish. As assistant to the minister she could have supplemented him in many ways within a framework of administration that he could have provided. But constant and frequent failures in the field of administration, with consequent severe criticism, finally drove this fine woman from church work entirely. There certainly is a place for a rich ministry of professionally trained women in the life of the church, but within any particular situation the channels for her service will need to be shaped in line with her personal qualities and her skills, and not in line with any preconceived institutional categories of service or any fixed notion as to the specific service for which the college or seminary is supposed to have trained her. In fact, the schools cannot afford her a " trade school " preparation, nor is this sort of " practical " training any assurance of success.

VIII

OTHER STAFF POSITIONS

One manifestation of our institutionalism in recent years is the rapid increase in the number of church *business managers*. These administrators are dedicated laymen who thus seek to fulfill their sense of Christian vocation and to perform an important Christian service. I shall not attempt an exhaustive discussion of their functions. A number of good books on church management are available. My purpose is to indicate briefly some of the points at which their impact on the total church is highly significant to other staff.

At the risk of seeming negative or critical I shall point to some problems and some dangers. The very excellent services of most of these churchmen may be assumed.

First of all, it is a false dichotomy, a fatal compromise with secularism, and a betrayal of the church to separate institutional matters from total ministry. The business management of a church is part of its witness and its ministry. Pastors say: " I let my laymen and the business manager tend to the business of the church so I am free to attend to spiritual matters." If the business of the church as an institution is not also " spiritual " and a part of its total life and ministry, then surely its witness will be greatly impaired.

So here is the first caution. Far too often the reputation of the manager is built on his ability to save money and protect plant and equipment. Therefore, he may be tempted continually to press for favors and discounts in purchasing, sometimes to the point of destroying the church's reputation for fair dealing. The church ought to be above reproach in dealing with the business world, and it ought to pay its way. Saving money is not a first consideration.

The care of buildings and equipment is important. But as watchdog over buildings and equipment, the manager may greatly please the trustees who know little about church activities, while seriously hampering the work of other staff and deterring lay participation. Church buildings are like a home for the congregation, and members should feel at home there. Reasonable wear and tear should be expected, as in a home. Leaders should feel free to drop in to meet with fellow workers, " to set up their rooms " for Sunday, to change church school displays. Yet we have seen such use drop sharply under the efficiency regime of a business manager. Good business, but poor psychology! The housewife who insists on keeping her house in perfect order and is upset by all wear and tear will find her own children down the street at a neighbor's home where there is freedom. Teachers who have to go to an office to get a key for a locked classroom or closet, and who feel that they are constantly checked in the use of equipment, will simply stay away. Children and young people react the same way. The physical property is well kept. The use is curtailed.

This is not to say that reasonable care is not desirable.

It is to say, however, that a business manager must understand and sympathize with program, and help to make the church buildings inviting to those whose interest and activity is essential.

An " efficient " church office is an abomination. When the business manager has made the office " businesslike," he has often destroyed its flavor as a church office. A good church office is at the heart of the church's life. It is a point of contact, a through-the-week face for the church, a symbol of accessibility and outreach. It is " social " and it is personal.

It is not very " efficient " for a secretary to talk over the telephone for fifteen minutes to old Mrs. Jones whenever she calls, but it may be important. An overly efficient office tends to repel the parishioner. Furthermore, secretaries who are regimented and supervised in the interest of business efficiency may soon lose the motivation of Christian service and church concern and become mere office workers. The " plus " is gone.

High use, a feeling on the part of members of the congregation that their church building belongs to them, freedom with accountability on the part of volunteer lay workers, the cultivation in children and youth of responsibility for proper use of what belongs to the " family " — all these may be, and sometimes are, undermined by the efforts of a dedicated manager, seeking to please a board who can only read ledgers and balance sheets. Watching the price of meals, the number of pencils used in the church school, the use of paper, the productivity of secretaries, and the industry of caretakers may be necessary and it may even be good stewardship. But the motive, the spirit, the method, by which these things are done will make a great deal of difference.

In a multiple staff situation, especially in large churches, a business manager with the ear of the pastor and of the official boards may come to " outrank " all other staff members and to constantly harass them in their work. Use of building and equipment, purchase of certain supplies for activities, cost of food and restrictions on service, deployment of secretarial help, may affect assistants much more directly than they affect the pastor. And more than one minister of Christian education has found his standing with boards subtly undermined by the evaluation and interpretation of a business manager who had little understanding of program and little understanding of how to work with volunteer leaders or with children and youth.

If one wants to get the whole story of the contribution of a business manager in a particular church, he will inquire not alone of pastor and trustees but of those staff members directly concerned with activities. The popularity of the manager often stops with the former.

May I say again that I do not condemn church business managers. They may often be victims of the false application of secular standards to the institutional phases of what is essentially an organism: the household of faith. But I do not mind being on record as viewing the trend to business managers as by no means an unmixed blessing. The business management of the church is a part of its ministry and its witness. It cannot be judged by standards other than those by which the whole life of the church is judged. Therefore, the business manager must be a churchman with deep insights into the meaning of mission and an understanding of program through which the church seeks to fulfill its mission. The employment of a manager adds an element to multiple staff relationships that must always be considered in evaluating those relationships.

The business manager must be a part of total staff, subject to the same supervision as other staff, accountable to the same board to which pastor and other staff are accountable. Whereas only his business experience and training may interest those concerned with the financial and material matters of the church, his character, Christian commitment, church experience, and ability to work with others should receive the same keen scrutiny given to a prospective assistant pastor or other staff member. He should understand that the material assets of the church as institution exist for no other reason than to serve its people in whatever ways their program purposes may indicate.

There are a sufficient number of instances in which the *choir director* is a disturber of staff relationships to warrant some brief treatment of the subject. And there are certainly many instances in which the choir director needs to be much more related to staff planning.

In the first place, a considerable number of choir directors are still not full-time church workers. Church music supplements a career in public-school music, private instruction, or another vocation. Too often choir directors have a superficial knowledge of church worship and church music and are without very deep understanding of the church, without theological insight, and even without deep commitment to the Christian faith. They are " directors " in the performing arts. Yet they demand and get a disciplined response from volunteers that no other staff member can command! And they often receive preferential treatment over other subordinate staff.

Sometimes the choir director, because of his functions in corporate worship, sustains a relationship to the pastor that is not accorded to any other staff member. As an artist in a field essential to the pastor, but in which the pastor is not knowledgeable or proficient, the choir director is handled with diplomatic courtesy, whereas other staff members have no such immunity. Also, as one who shares the spotlight with the preacher Sunday after Sunday, the choir director sustains a different relationship to the congregation from that of other staff assistants. His problems in human relationships are often critical, yet no demands comparable to those made upon assistant ministers or D.C.E.'s are made upon him. For example, in one church in which there were frequent staff disruptions, an arbitrary and dictatorial choir director was tolerated for years because he was able to bring a choir to near-perfect performance.

I have known not a few instances in which the choir director with a flair for high-class performance received a good deal of praise and public acclaim never accorded to a hard-working director of Christian education whose work load and whose problems far overshadowed those of the choir director. This discrimination has been sometimes an occasion for jealousy and often a cause of great discouragement.

But it is when the choir director is responsible for developing children's and youth choirs that most tension is likely to develop. He may be that rare churchman who sees that participation in music is an integral part of the Christian nurture of youth and but one aspect of their total experience of worship and service in the life of the congregation. Or he may be the practitioner of an art for whom the show is the all-important matter. If the performance is the important aim, the choir director must have the children for rehearsal and performance without regard to other activities and schedules. The child is a pawn subjected to competing demands.

No pastor or church committee can afford to ignore the matter of the integration of music training into the total Christian education program and the harmonious working together of those whose leadership involves the same persons. Frequent instances come to light in which, in times of conflict, a worship and music committee has little or no communication with the Christian education committee. The minister or director of Christian education, together with the volunteers related to him or to her, usually superintendents and teachers in several departments of the church school, are in a cold war with the director of choirs. In these cases the welfare of the children is paramount. They belong to the church and not to any particular department or activity.

Music is a way to spiritual enrichment. Of fundamental importance in Reformed worship is the singing congregation, not the performing choir. Music for the child or youth is integral to his Christian nurture. Singing and a knowledge of music should be considered as enriching his total experience as a participant in the life and worship of the church. The aim is not perfection in performance for an admiring audience. Therefore, choir directors should be a part of total staff, subject to the same guiding principles of service and the same educational standards as all other members of staff. They should meet with staff, at least on occasion, and this planning with staff should be a condition of their part-time employment even if they are paid extra for time and travel expense. They should know the other staff members much more intimately than is often the case and they should be better acquainted with the total program. They should be more concerned with what happens in music throughout the church program, not only in corporate worship. Too often the music standards in church school departments are anything but equal in quality—musically, artistically, or theologically—with those maintained in corporate worship. When a church is proud of the high quality of church music evident in its corporate worship, it is somewhat startling to find in its church school a continuous struggle to prevent the infiltration of music that is indefensible by good standards.

A very important person in the local church's life and work is the person variously known as *janitor, caretaker, custodian, or sexton.* Proficiency, as a skilled workman, in keeping a church plant in good running order, essential as it is, comes close to being the least of his virtues. From long experience I know how the caretaker can support the work of staff, especially those who direct daily activities in and about the buildings, and I know how a grudging and uncooperative caretaker can damage morale and cause friction.

The sexton is a public relations personage. His countless weekly contacts with volunteer leaders, with children, and with youth are highly significant. He can by his cheerful and helpful attitude endear himself to teachers, to officers of women's groups, and to staff members for whose comfort and convenience he manifests some concern. In his relationship to children and youth the sexton always is the most influential person in determining their attitude toward the use and care of the church building and equipment. Their attitudes toward him will be subtly reflected in their response to other leaders in activities that occur at the church building. His attitudes have much to do with "discipline."

The sexton who understands program and has some feeling for the convenience of the church school teachers, and some regard for the supplies and equipment that are so important to them, will make an excellent contribution to the morale of these volunteers, thereby greatly assisting other staff members who are engaged in the recruiting and in supervision of workers. So important is the attitude of the sexton to the program that his work must be evaluated from this point of view as well as from that of mere efficiency in custodial services. Sometimes discontent on the part of staff members and volunteer workers has to reach major proportions before trustees or building committees will recognize the problem. In one instance a director of Christian education had to present her resignation, expressing through that act the rising indignation of her teaching staff, before the trustees would act with regard to a caretaker who was uncooperative and often abusive. The attitude of the trustees was that he took good care of the building at minimum cost and that they could not see the relationship between his attitudes and the work of teachers and other leaders.

Since it is unfair to expect the sexton to take orders from everyone, a staff should work out clear channels of communication. The sexton should be thoroughly briefed about the schedule and the plans for activities. He should be given every help in properly planning his work. Every care should be taken not to unnecessarily add to his burdens, and all staff members should be concerned for saving the extra steps and extra efforts that may be carelessly demanded. The sexton should feel that he rates as part of the staff, and that the need for him to understand and sympathize with the program is reciprocated by understanding of his work load and of the importance of his cooperation.

IX

"IN HONOR PREFERRING ONE ANOTHER"

In spite of the problems that are involved, multiple staffs open up ample opportunities for enriching the ministry and the life of the church. The critical question has been stated or implied often in the preceding chapters. It is: Are we determined to deepen the ministry or merely to extend the institutional church? Are we committed to pioneering on new frontiers or merely to improving our capacities for doing more of the same? In other words, does more staff simply mean more calling, more group meetings, more committee meetings, more promotion, more mailings and telephoning, more effort to do for people what they should do for themselves? Or does it mean better preaching, more teaching, more counseling, more penetrative evangelism, more long-range, systematic leadership recruitment and training on the basis of accepted standards and clearly enunciated purposes?

The success of multiple ministry in the years ahead depends greatly upon an intensified study of the meaning of the ministry. "The purpose of the church and its ministry," to quote the title of a book that every multiple staff group should study together, must become the deep concern of each multiple staff. The institutional criteria for the success of the church must be kept in proper perspective, subservient to the charismatic purposes. The church is an organism, whatever else it may appear to be. It is more like a family than like any other institution. It is a community intensely dynamic and vibrant, interacting within itself and with the world around it. Church order uses organization, or structure, but church order is not the same as organization. Order comes from common purpose, mutual responsibility, disciplined freedom. It demands trust and loyalty. Order cannot really be imposed but must be created by those who are to be set free by it, and to act responsibly within it. Christian order grows out of mutually acknowledged dependence and interdependence. It depends upon mutually accepted agreements and understandings, which give the essential security and the necessary framework for action.

It is in relationship to this concept of the church as organism that a unity of ministry is required. *The integrity of the organism dictates the unity of ministry.*

Webster defines "organism" as follows: Biology — "An individual constituted to carry on the activities of life by means of parts or organs more or less separate in function but mutually dependent." Metaphysics — "Any thing, structure, or totality of correlative parts, in which the relationship of part to part involves a relationship of part to whole, thus making it self-inclusive and self-dependent. Kant defines an organism as a material being 'which is possible only through the relation of all that is contained in it to something else as end and means.'"

It is certain that Paul had not read Webster, but who can doubt that Paul had the concept of the church as organism as he wrote to the Romans (Rom., ch. 12) or to the Corinthians (I Cor., ch. 12) or to the Ephesians (Eph., ch. 4). He speaks of diversity of gifts in the one body. He was addressing a congregation and not a church staff when he wrote " speaking the truth in love, we are to grow up in every way into him who is the head, into Christ, from whom the whole body, joined and knit together by every joint with which it is supplied, when each part is working properly, makes bodily growth and upbuilds itself in love." But Paul might well have been writing to a church staff, for if this kind of unity is to be manifest in the congregation, it certainly must be a matter of daily witness among those who are to lead the congregation.

And so we repeat: the integrity of the organism dictates the unity of ministry.

I do not mean to imply that the concept of organism fully describes the particular church in which a staff must serve. The church is a part of secular societies. It is a truly human community, partaking of all the weaknesses and foibles of being in the world. But the church must understand itself from within. And until we have honestly and earnestly and prayerfully tried to understand the church in the light of God's purposes we have no right to make the compromises that our human limitations seem to demand. Indeed, we are not able to make compromises wisely and well except under the constant challenge of the ideal. It is the tendency, so often observed, to make largely institutional and secular evaluations and judgments in multiple staff problems, against which I am contending.

Recognition of this unity which responds to order is basic to freedom in diversity of function. This diversity is not basically an institutional diversity, but a diversity of personal qualities, talents, skills, and accepted areas of emphasis. In other words, the diversity that is possible within unity comes from an acceptance of this basic unity of the ministry before any concessions are made to the practical demands of institutional complexity.

This unity of ministry recognizes that we deal with whole persons within a dynamic community, a community within which the paramount consideration is the relationship of persons to God in Christ, and to each other as a consequence of their commitment to God. The nature of the church as organism and the unity of the ministry in and through the church suggest that no one should be called to a particular phase of the church's work to be isolated or protected in it. No one can ultimately sustain a fruitful ministry in a particular phase of church life apart from a vital relationship to all other phases. As the health of the whole depends upon the health of all the parts in this organism, so must any particular ministry be properly related to all ministries. This demands attention to the meaning of order as a foundation for staff operations. There is an analogy that helps to explain the meaning of order as I am using the term. A layman once asked me to clarify for him what I mean by saying that order is something different from and deeper than mere organization. Knowing that he had a fine family of four children, I asked, " Is your family well-organized? " He hesitated and then said, " Perhaps in some ways, but sometimes I don't think so." " Why don't you organize it? " I asked. " You are an experienced business executive; surely you can organize your own family.

" But you do have order in your family and that order depends on some pretty fundamental things. It depends upon commonly understood and accepted purposes, and common agreements, often unspoken. It depends upon mutual love and trust. All sorts of means of communication prevail, possible only in a context of understanding, acceptance, and trust. There is a common language that is a family language. Dependability and responsible action are manifest. If the children had no agreed-upon bedtime; if they never knew when meals would be ready; if they never knew whether Mother would be home when they returned from school; if they were never sure when Dad would come home; then indeed disorder would be disastrously evident. If they could never speak of joy and sorrow and have them shared; if error could not be corrected and then forgiven; if discipline had no rhyme or reason — then indeed there would be no order.

"For these things are basic and no fresh rules made up each day, no good housekeeping, no correct diets or exemplary rules of health, no correct and dispassionate refereeing of quarrels, would ever bring order. Whatever might properly be called organization in the commonly understood sense would be only a means to which order is prior and absolutely essential. Organization without order for a time obscures and then compounds chaos."

Within the Christian community, which we call church, status and preference cannot rightly be bestowed. Attempts to bestow power or status or to usurp them are always ultimately corrupting. But honor, love, loyalty, the power to influence by example, may be earned. A power struggle between members of a staff is always destructive of the unity of the ministry and ultimately of the health of the organism.

There should be a "chief of staff." But to be the head of a staff is a responsibility, a burden, and not a privilege. It is a way of working and not a way of showing power or preference. There is a very grave doubt whether there should be staff titles that suggest roles. Actually, for a properly unified staff within a congregation whose leaders have come to understand diversity of function within unity, titles are not necessary for those who understand; for those who do not understand, the titles are vastly misleading anyway. Does " minister of Christian education " mean that this assistant pastor is an educator, a teacher, or that he " runs " those activities obviously meant to be educational, such as the church school? Does it mean that the pastor is no longer educator or teacher? What better way to buck the concept that the whole church teaches and that the total life of the church is the framework of its nurture than by identifying this title with restricted areas of activity? And so would it not be better to dispense with all titles in terms of function or roles, as some churches have done, and refer to each person as a minister of the church?

Daniel Day Williams has written (*The Minister and the Care of Souls,* page 50; Harper & Brothers, 1961) : " When we speak of authority in the Christian faith and ministry, we must see that authority through its source in the revelation of Jesus Christ. This is to say that our authority derives from Him whose claim rests finally on nothing other than the sheer expression of love to God and to men. We do not agree in the Christian church about the proper forms of authority in the ministry; but whatever they may be, we cannot escape the truth that God in his decisive word to us has left us no ultimate reliance upon institution or tradition save that which arises from personal trust in Him." Daily the personal relationships of persons in a multiple staff stand under the judgment of the gospel to which they have made commitment and for which they have become responsible in word and deed.

Ministers within a multiple staff must live realistically

and honestly with the truth that we are all sinners. We must daily face the fact of sin in our human relationships. We do have hostilities; we are jealous; we do react to hurts with something less than magnanimity and forgiveness. We do find it difficult to take second place; we do practice self-deception; we do love praise and power. The image of the " good " man which we hold, and which our people thrust upon us, prevents unmasking. The man in the mirror is seen through colored glasses.

Perhaps a basic consideration for good staff relationships would be the recognition of the need for each minister to be a minister, a priest if you will, to his fellow minister. How often it appears that members of a staff have not thought seriously about serving and supporting each other, about learning from each other, " in honor preferring one another." If an older man has wisdom and experience to share with a younger assistant, so a young assistant often has fresh views of theology, or newer concepts of education, a knowledge of new books, and certain skills (for instance, a knowledge of group process) that the older minister should welcome. And if an assistant is burdened with activity so that his study is neglected, why should not the preaching minister, out of his study and preparation, bring stimulation and continued learning to his assistant?

Sharing in multiple staff is a two-way street. This is often not recognized. An assistant, bothered perhaps by lack of status, or by the ineptitude with which the senior pastor handles staff relations, may complain bitterly, may build up resentments and hostility. How often does he try to accept the " boss " as a person, to see how much the older man may be bound by his self-image or the image that his congregation has created for him? Does the assistant accept his responsibility to react to a situation in a mature manner, without recrimination or blame? Above all, will he seek to discover the basis of his own insecurity or hostility? In not a few cases in which an assistant has sought counseling following staff difficulties, he has found that deep-seated resentment toward " taking orders " dating back into his childhood is part of the problem. And in cases in which a young assistant resents the " fatherly " concern of an older pastor, the difficulty often stems from a conflict with his own father.

We have stated above that the members of a multiple staff should study together. This common study and discussion is not only a good discipline in relationships but it is a way to establish the common ground or base from which to operate. For instance, to give a practical example first, it is not unusual to find an older pastor who, through a long succession of assistants charged with responsibility for education, has not read a book on Christian education or attended a class or an institute or a school for many years. He presumes to judge instantly the point of view and the work of the assistant in a field in which he is not even so well informed as some of his lay leaders. Static views of the church and of its ministry are bad enough under any circumstances; they become an endless source of trouble in staff relationships.

Just as a suggestion, I will give a list of books that may be studied and discussed together in multiple staffs. Anyone who has read this far will scarcely have the nerve to say that there is no time for this essential step toward harmony and productivity in staff relationships. Time must be found! Quite naturally, different persons would suggest different books. But there are categories or areas that should be represented: theology, the nature of the church, the nature of the ministry, Christian education, evangelism, stewardship, and ways of dealing with persons.

To include a book list has its dangers. I trust that much of the material of this book will not be outdated for many a year; a book list will seem to many to be out of date by the time it is published. But this brief list of books of proved value will readily suggest others to pastors.

1. *The Constitution* (especially the Form of Government and the Directory for Worship) and *The Book of Common Worship.* (There are similar documents for each denomination.)

Few ministers are sufficiently versed in these basic documents. Men come out of seminary with insufficient training in polity, and pastors become rusty in their understanding, interpretation, and use of polity. Ministers may differ in interpretation of important aspects of church government. We are not concerned for legalism but for the creative use of tradition and for the disciplines in which our freedom is protected.

2. *The Purpose of the Church and Its Ministry,* H. Richard Niebuhr (Harper & Brothers, 1956). Said a reviewer of this classic: " There are no more singing pages in all Protestant theology than are to be found in this book." It sets forth in inspired and inspiring style the deep insights of Professor Niebuhr concerning the church, sharpened and informed by his experience as director of the Study of Theological Education in the United States and Canada. No pastor could seriously study this book without careful evaluation of his ministry. Especially valuable is the discussion of the authority of the minister: the bases of his communal authority as he understands and lives within tradition.

3. *The Church Redemptive,* Howard Grimes (Abingdon Press, 1958). With excellent use of various sources,

the author discusses the nature of the church, and then deals with the various aspects of the church's life and work against the background of this understanding of what the church is. Study of this book by the staff and then by groups of lay leaders will help to clarify the central purposes that should mark all activities.

4. *Treasure in Earthen Vessels: The Church as a Human Community,* James Gustafson (Harper & Brothers, 1961). This book is an important contribution toward an understanding of the church from a sociological point of view and as a part of secular societies. It will help to sustain a high doctrine of the church, while facing honestly its character as a human community. One great value of the book is its many references to basic sources, making it an excellent guide to further study.

5. *The Recovery of the Teaching Ministry,* J. Stanley Glen (The Westminster Press, 1960). If this book will not jar ministers awake to their teaching responsibility, perhaps nothing will. It sets the teaching task in proper perspective, as absolutely essential to effective proclamation, and it will set all other tasks of the minister in better perspective.

6. *The Gift of Power,* Lewis Sherrill (The Macmillan Company, 1957). This is not a simple book. One may almost say that into it are packed the fruits of a lifetime of study and teaching which made Dr. Sherrill outstanding among educators of this generation. The book deals with the theological foundations of Christian nurture and is rich in insights not only as to how human growth and change take place but also as to the kind of redemptive fellowship the Christian community must come to be.

7. *A Philosophy of Adult Christian Education,* David Ernsberger (The Westminster Press, 1959). Ernsberger

writes very helpfully and practically on the role of the minister, including his responsibility as educator. His discussion of adult education in the church gives valuable guidance not only in those specifics commonly recognized as adult education but in the kind of ordering of church life that is conducive to adult learning and growth.

8. *The Meaning of Persons,* Paul Tournier, trans. Edwin Hudson (Harper & Brothers, 1957). This book has been of great help to many ministers, not only in self-understanding but in helping other persons. Among other things, it deals with a problem particularly acute in the ministry, namely, the conflict between the person (what one really is as a person) and the personage (what he may conceive himself to be or what others assume him to be). The book throws great light on the roots of wholesome relationships.

9. *The Minister and the Care of Souls,* Daniel Day Williams (Harper & Brothers, 1961). The chapters " Forgiveness, Judgment, and Acceptance " and " The Minister's Self-knowledge " are especially helpful. Williams brings to his writing a fruitful parish experience, years of experience as a seminary teacher, and his research as associate director with Dr. Richard Niebuhr of the Study of Theological Education in the United States and Canada. He edited with Dr. Niebuhr *The Ministry in Historical Perspectives* (Harper & Brothers, 1956), which is also a source of valuable insights as to the nature of the ministry.

10. *The Rebirth of Ministry,* James D. Smart (The Westminster Press, 1960). This study of the " Biblical character of the church's ministry " discusses the minister as preacher, teacher, pastor, theologian, and evangelist, all essential components of a whole ministry. Smart does not forget that a " whole ministry " involves the laity.

Much as I believe in a continuing education for the minister, these books are not suggested, let us be reminded, for that purpose only; rather, they are suggested for study together and as a basis of discussion in the interest of a meeting of minds and a fellowship in understanding and in work.

X

BY WAY OF SUMMARY

1. *Why a Multiple Staff?* The basic question to be asked by a church calling multiple staff is: Is it our intention to deepen the ministry of the church or to extend the institution?

The purpose and the meaning of ministry is essentially no different for a staff of two, or five, or ten, than for a staff of one. More staff can do more things, and that very fact makes critical judgment more necessary and more severe. Increased activity is not the primary test. A church cannot hire enough staff to make a great church, else the richest would easily be the best. And not a few churches are actually impoverished or hindered by the addition of staff. If there is no clarity of purpose, no good and viable self-image, no clear goals, addition of staff may merely compound the confusion and for a time hide lack of wholeness and health.

2. *Administration Is a Relative Factor.* Administration efficient from an institutional point of view is by no means a guarantee of a satisfactory multiple staff ministry. A pastor who is a well-organized, decisive, directive administra-

tor may lack perception in developing the deeper levels of a shared ministry and in discerning the quality of relationships to persons that should characterize the ministry of his assistants. He may make a too-largely " administrative " evaluation of that ministry. The qualities of administration that will provide the framework and the proper points of reference for productive multiple ministry may escape the pastor as administrator, no matter how gifted he may be in the charismatic aspects of his own ministry, if he does not accommodate himself to the new dimensions that are present with multiple staff. The fact is that church administration for multiple staff is in many ways more complex than in the case of the single pastor. This is not chiefly due to greater size and more activity. It is due to the fact that church administration, to be in keeping with the nature and the mission of the church, must grow out of the nature of the ministry and must not be dictated by secular institutional standards. And that ministry is or should become richer and more complex and more pervasive in a multiple staff.

3. *The Unstructured Situation.* In contrast to, or at least different from, the strongly administered church as a context for multiple staff operations is the church that has been ruled with a charismatic accent or by what has been called a " pastoral " approach. The pastor may lead by the prestige of position, by persuasion, by personal example, or by means of the loyalties he commands by virtue of his personal qualities of mind and spirit. That the organization seems often at loose ends is sometimes annoying but seldom crucial. In this situation there are important considerations to be faced. First, the pastor must recognize the nature of his leadership or his " rule," its strengths and

its limitations. If he cannot admit any ineptitude in administration, he will attempt, under the stress of multiple staff problems, administrative innovations for which he has little talent. On the other hand, he must recognize that an assistant cannot successfully fulfill his functions by " playing it by ear " or by intuitive expediency, as the pastor may have done. The channels of communication and the lines of responsibility must now be made clearer. The pastor must allow more structure to be developed, and he must be willing to accept the effect of that additional structure upon his own exercise of power and responsibility. Also, an assistant with a flare for organization and administration must understand and accept the existing conditions. Otherwise he may tend to create his own following and introduce strains into the order which no one clearly understands; or he may come into sharp conflict on matters of policy; or he may create an administrative structure not properly related to the whole. He may tend to work through committees and officers not properly related to the central power structure, which the pastor controls. Worst of all, he may fail utterly to understand and appreciate the real strengths of the pastor's leadership and simply break himself against what he considers an inertia that he has failed to comprehend.

4. *Order and Organization.* Good church order is not to be equated with what appears to be effective institutional organization. They are not incompatible but they do not always exist together. A highly organized church — one with constitution, bylaws, boards, committees, procedures, activities, promotion — may be sadly lacking in church order. Good church order means a people consciously under the rule of Word and Sacrament. It means

a high sense of mission, a sense of wholeness and community, awareness of common purposes and goals. It means disciplined freedom. Wrote Bryan Green (*The Practice of Evangelism,* page 45; Charles Scribner's Sons, 1951): " All that the church does concerns all her members, and they all have some share in every part of her total life." In the well-ordered church this is obvious and becomes the central fact of worship and work. Such good order is basic to a shared ministry. A successful and satisfying multiple staff operation can seldom be maintained without a constant effort to understand, develop, and maintain such order. The necessary structure and organizational or administrative procedures can be built on this base. Without it all sorts of administrative and organizational manipulation ultimately ends in frustration or at least in a vast misdirection and misuse of the true gifts of ministry.

5. *The Pastor Should Review His Own Ministry.* Before calling the first assistant, and preferably each time an assistant is to be called, the pastor should carefully review and evaluate his own ministry and lead his boards and committees in an evaluation of the entire program. The coming of an assistant inevitably affects the pastor's role, and each assistant affects it differently. Better that the impact be anticipated, accepted, and guided in creative fashion than that it occur by chance or default. The pastor may well use the advent of new staff as an occasion for reform and revitalization of his own ministry. If he goes on in the same manner as before, he is in danger of simply adding to his burdens; or shifting without plan the items of concern for which he should remain chiefly responsible; or giving to the assistant those things which he has neglected, or does not like, or in which he has largely failed

— all without the correlation essential to his own continuing work or that of his assistant. A large amount of disappointing performance can be traced to the failure of a senior pastor to reform his own ministry and to lead his boards to see that they call staff to a united and shared ministry, no matter what specific assignment may be accepted, and not simply compartmentalize aspects of institutional activity.

6. *A Year of Preparation.* A church calling an assistant for the first time should devote a year to preparation. A pastor and the responsible lay leaders cannot act intelligently without study and evaluation, and often they cannot find the right man without patient search. It is important that the congregation be prepared through careful interpretation of needs, purposes, and realistic goals. The fact that there are so many false starts as churches enter the multiple staff phase, and that some go on making mistake after mistake, is proof enough of the need of a better strategy. Trial and error is costly and it is not necessary. One of the great needs of the church is the development of experienced counseling services in making this evaluation and in calling staff.

7. *Each Addition Affects All Staff.* Addition of staff calls for a review of total staff operation. Of especial importance is the review of secretarial services. Adjustments of secretarial service is often a bone of contention. The notion that "we will work it out some way" after the assistant comes, or "he can use volunteer help," or worse yet, "he will not have much need of secretarial help," has been a stumbling block in the path of many a new staff venture. Secretarial help is essential in the modern church, at least

in an urban situation. It is a good investment. I would strongly advise in many instances not to call additional staff until the secretarial situation is reformed both as to quantity and quality.

8. *Business Management Is a Part of Ministry.* The business administration of a church should be oriented toward ministry and mission and not toward secular business. This does not obviate sound business practice. The business of the church is ministry and its " business " is a part of its ministry. The qualifications of a business manager certainly must accent managerial training and experience but churchmanship and understanding of program are equally important. The all-around churchmanship and the Christian maturity and commitment of a business manager is almost of equal importance with that of the pastor, not only for his own satisfaction in Christian service, but for the effectiveness of other staff whose ministry he affects in so many direct and subtle ways.

9. *Job Descriptions for All Staff.* If job descriptions are to be worked out for new staff members, they are generally more or less unsatisfactory unless properly related to similar job descriptions for all members of the staff. If they are couched in vague generalities, as is often the case, they are open to wide differences of interpretation. Even the best of them should be flexible guides to a creative process for realizing the greatest potentials of training and talents, and should be subject to frequent review and revision.

10. *Staff Family Relationships.* Wives are an important factor in staff relationships. In calling an assistant pastor, the church must consider his wife in relation to the situa-

tion. The situation certainly includes the pastor's wife: her relationships to his work and to the activities of the church, her attitude, her role in the congregation. A shared ministry cannot leave family relationships out of account.

11. *Staff Interpersonal Relations Are Critical.* A productive multiple ministry, which is to make possible the greatest possible use of each man's gifts and a richer ministry because of their teamwork, demands that every effort be made to establish and to maintain deep foundations for the staff members' relationships to one another as persons and as ministers. There is no substitute for this foundation. Failure at this point, far too often observed, inevitably detracts from the fullest use of the gifts and the training and the experience of each one. And it affects the life of the congregation in corrosive ways not unlike those in which the breakdown of husband and wife relationships disturb the lives and relationships of children. The nature of the church as organism demands the unity of ministry. If ministers cannot establish and maintain open, honest, accepting, and supportive relationships, they have written a large factor of failure into their service together in the church.

This is a fresh and creative approach to one of the major practical problems confronting local churches of all denominations. It is an analysis of the interrelationships that constantly face people who are members of the full-time staff of the church. Guidance is given in evaluating typical situations, and suggestions are made that lead to insight and understanding. Dr. Sweet spells out the basic issues in staff relationships, and examines various " philosophies " of administration with respect to their effect upon staff functioning.

Attention is given to the varied considerations by which the pastor and church leaders commonly determine when staff is needed and for what purpose, what roles must be defined, and what types of training, aptitude, and experience should be considered in searching for additional staff. Critical examination is given to the varied and often ill-considered reasons that may motivate a church in calling additional staff, and sharp questions are raised about the value of multiple staff in some situations.